T0210829

Lecture Notes in Computer Science   12386

More information about this series at http://www.springer.com/series/7410

Kostantinos Markantonakis ·
Marinella Petrocchi (Eds.)

Security and Trust Management

16th International Workshop, STM 2020
Guildford, UK, September 17–18, 2020
Proceedings

 Springer

Editors
Kostantinos Markantonakis
Royal Holloway, University of London
Egham, UK

Marinella Petrocchi 🄳
National Research Council
Pisa, Italy

ISSN 0302-9743   ISSN 1611-3349   (electronic)
Lecture Notes in Computer Science
ISBN 978-3-030-59816-7   ISBN 978-3-030-59817-4   (eBook)
https://doi.org/10.1007/978-3-030-59817-4

LNCS Sublibrary: SL4 – Security and Cryptology

This Springer imprint is published by the registered company Springer Nature Switzerland AG
The registered company address is: Gewerbestrasse 11, 6330 Cham, Switzerland

Preface

These proceedings contain the papers selected for presentation at the 16th International Workshop on Security and Trust Management (STM 2020) held as an online event during September 17–18, 2020, in conjunction with the 25th European Symposium on Research in Computer Security (ESORICS 2020). After evaluating the ongoing COVID-19 situation, the decision was made to run ESORICS 2020 and the associated workshops as an all-digital conference experience. Therefore, STM 2020 took place as an entirely virtual event.

In response to the call for papers, 20 papers were submitted to the workshop. These papers were evaluated based on their significance, novelty, and technical quality. As in previous years, reviewing was double-blind: The identities of reviewers were not revealed to the authors of the papers and identities of authors were not revealed to the reviewers.

The Program Committee meeting was held electronically, yielding intensive discussion over two weeks.

Of the papers submitted, eight were selected for presentation at the conference (an acceptance rate of 40%).

The workshop also included two invited talks, one by Professor Ernesto Damiani and one by Jorge Luis Toro Pozo, the winner of the 2020 ERCIM WG STM Best PhD Thesis Award.

An event like this does not just happen; it depends on the volunteer efforts of a host of individuals. There is a long list of people who volunteered their time and energy to put together the workshop and who deserve special recognition.

Thanks to all the members of the Program Committee and the external reviewers. Their hard work in the paper evaluation is much appreciated.

We are also very grateful to all those people whose work ensured a smooth organization process: Pierangela Samarati, chair of the Security and Trust Management Working Group, for her support and advice; Steve Schneider, for his support as general chair of ESORICS 2020; Mark Manulis, for his help as workshop chair of ESORICS 2020; Darren Hurley-Smith, for taking care of publicity; and Michela Fazzolari, for taking care of the workshop website.

Last, but certainly not least, thanks go to all the authors who submitted papers, and to all the attendees who contributed to the workshop discussions. We hope all readers and attendees find the proceedings stimulating and a source of inspiration for future research and practical development work.

August 2020

Kostantinos Markantonakis
Marinella Petrocchi

Organization

Program Chairs

Kostantinos Markantonakis	Royal Holloway, UK
Marinella Petrocchi	CNR, Italy

Publicity Chair

Darren Hurley-Smith	Royal Holloway, UK

Web Chair

Michela Fazzolari	CNR, Italy

STM Steering Committee

Pierangela Samarati (Chairperson)	University of Milan, Italy
Theo Dimitrakos	British Telecom, UK
Javier Lopez	University of Malaga, Spain
Fabio Martinelli	CNR, Italy
Sjouke Mauw	University of Luxembourg, Luxembourg
Stig F. Mjølsnes	Norwegian University of Science and Technology, Norway
Ulrich Ultes-Nitsche	University of Fribourg, Switzerland

Program Committee

Sara Abugazalah	King Khalid University, Saudi Arabia
Raja Naeem Akram	Royal Holloway, UK
Cristina Alcaraz	University of Malaga, Spain
Stefano Calzavara	Università Ca' Foscari, Italy
Lorenzo Cavallaro	King's College, UK
Madeline Cheah	Horiba Mira, UK
Mauro Conti	University of Padua, Italy
Gabriele Costa	IMT Lucca, Italy
Haitham Cruickshank	University of Surrey, UK
Jorge Cuellar	Siemens AG, Germany
Sabrina De Capitani di Vimercati	University of Milan, Italy
Rocco De Nicola	IMT Lucca, Italy
Roberto Di Pietro	Hamad Bin Khalifa University, Qatar

Michela Fazzolari	CNR, Italy
Sara Foresti	University of Milan, Italy
Letterio Galletta	IMT Lucca, Italy
Olga Gadyatskaya	Leiden University, The Netherlands
Gerhard Hancke	City University of Hong Kong, Hong Kong
Thibaut Heckmann	ISG Smart Card and IoT Security Centre, UK
Julio Hernandez	University of Kent, UK
Darren Hurley-Smith	Royal Holloway, UK
Christo Kaloniatis	University of the Aegean, Greece
Ghassan Karame	NEC Laboratories Europe, Germany
Niko Komninos	City University, UK
Giovanni Livraga	University of Milan, Italy
Eleonora Losiouk	University of Padua, Italy
Emmanuel Magkos	Ionian University, Greece
Luigi Mancini	University of Rome La Sapienza, Italy
Fabio Martinelli	CNR, Italy
Ilaria Matteucci	CNR, Italy
Sjouke Mauw	University of Luxembourg, Luxembourg
Keith Mayes	Royal Holloway, UK
Nikolaos Petroulakis	Foundation for Research and Technology-Hellas (FORTH), Greece
Nikos Pitropakis	Edinburgh Napier University, UK
Joachim Possega	University of Passau, Germany
Kostantinos Rantos	Eastern Macedonia and Thrace Institute of Technology, Greece
Michael Rusinowitch	LORIA, Inria Nancy, France
Pierangela Samarati	University of Milan, Italy
Damien Sauveron	University of Limoges, France
Daniele Sgandurra	Royal Holloway, UK
Angelo Spognardi	University of Rome La Sapienza, Italy
Mark Strembeck	Vienna University of Economics and Business, Austria
Tom Van Goethem	KU Leuven, Belgium
Mathy Vanhoef	NYU Abu Dhabi, UAE
Chan Yeob Yeun	Khalifa University, UAE
Chia-Mu Yu	National Chung Hsing University, Taiwan

External Reviewers

Andreina, Sebastien
Bakiras, Spiridon
Casagrande, Marco
D'Arco, Paolo
Papadopoulos, Pavlos

Contents

Security Properties and Attacks

Modelling of 802.11 4-Way Handshake Attacks and Analysis of Security Properties

Rajiv Ranjan Singh[1,2]([✉]) [iD], José Moreira[1] [iD], Tom Chothia[1],
and Mark D. Ryan[1]

[1] School of Computer Science, University of Birmingham, Birmingham, UK
{r.r.singh,j.moreira-sanchez,t.p.chothia,m.d.ryan}@cs.bham.ac.uk
[2] Department of Computer Science, Shyam Lal College (Eve.),
University of Delhi, Delhi, India
rrsingh@shyamlale.du.ac.in

Abstract. The IEEE 802.11 standard defines a 4-way handshake between a supplicant and an authenticator for secure communication. Many attacks such as KRACK, cipher downgrades, and key recovery attacks have been recently discovered against it. These attacks raise the question as to whether the implementation violates one of the required security properties or whether the security properties are insufficient. To the best of our knowledge, this is the first work that shows how to answer this question using formal methods. We model and analyse a variety of these attacks using the TAMARIN prover against the security properties mandated by the standard for the 4-way handshake. This lets us see which security properties are violated. We find that our TAMARIN models vulnerable to the KRACK attacks do not violate any of the standard's security properties, indicating that the properties, as specified by the standard, are insufficient. We propose an additional security property and show that it is violated by systems vulnerable to KRACK attacks, and that enforcing this property is successful in stopping them. We demonstrate how to use TAMARIN to automatically test the adequacy of a set of security properties against attacks, and that the suggested mitigations make 802.11 secure against these attacks.

Keywords: IEEE 802.11 · WPA2 · 4-way handshake · Group key handshake · KRACK attack · Downgrade attack · TAMARIN prover · SAPiC

1 Introduction

The IEEE 802.11 standard [3] defines a *4-way handshake* as the key management protocol. It involves exchanging four messages between an access point (AP) and a client, or equivalently in 802.11 terminology, an authenticator and a supplicant. These exchanges enables parties to compute and share session/group keys for future unicast/multicast secure communication over the wireless medium. It also provides mutual authentication and session-key agreement.

© Springer Nature Switzerland AG 2020
K. Markantonakis and M. Petrocchi (Eds.): STM 2020, LNCS 12386, pp. 3–21, 2020.
https://doi.org/10.1007/978-3-030-59817-4_1

The 4-way handshake was proven formally secure [13,14], and had no attacks published on it until recently, when the so-called Key Reinstallation Attack (KRACK) was uncovered by Vanhoef and Piessens in 2017 [22]. This attack exploits design and/or implementation flaws in the 4-way handshake by reinstalling already in-use session or group keys. As a consequence, the adversary can break the security guarantees, even with a secure protocol for data confidentiality, such as the AES-based Counter Cipher Mode with Block Chaining Message Authentication Code Protocol (AES-CCMP), and decrypt or replay messages [22].

Moreover, various 4-way handshake implementations have been found to be vulnerable to downgrade attacks in widely used routers [20], including models of Cisco and TP-Link. These attacks mostly affect the AP, when both the AP and the client support AES-CCMP and Temporal Key Integrity Protocol (TKIP) cipher suites. Although the client is always likely to choose the stronger AES-CCMP cipher suite over TKIP, an adversary can trick the AP into using TKIP.

We start our work by building models of 4-way handshake using the security protocol verification tool TAMARIN [18]. Our modelling focuses on the subset of functionalities and messages for successful execution of the attacks on 4-way handshake, and not building a complete model of the 802.11 state machines, thus enabling a Dolev-Yao adversary [11] to exploit the vulnerabilities. We show that TAMARIN can find the attacks mentioned above, and our models can formally verify that the suggested fixes to the vulnerabilities work as intended.

The IEEE 802.11 standard defines a list of security properties suggesting that it will lead to a secure 4-way handshake (e.g., freshness of session keys, secrecy of session/group keys, authentication). The existence of the attacks described above raises serious questions about these security properties: Does the IEEE 802.11 specification or some implementation violate these properties, leading to these attacks? Or are these security properties insufficient to guarantee security? If so, what security properties would be sufficient to stop the attacks? In this paper we show how these questions can be formally answered using TAMARIN.

We encode the security properties from the standard using TAMARIN, and use the tool to see if any of these security properties are violated in the presence of the attacks. We find that the weaknesses that lead to the KRACK attacks [22] *do not* violate any of the required properties. This suggests that the security properties, as defined in the standard, are insufficient. We then propose new security properties, and by imposing them as restrictions in TAMARIN, we show that ensuring these new suggested properties is enough to stop these attacks.

We remark that our approach here is different from the normal use of formal methods for checking security protocols, which consists in defining a model of a protocol with its security properties to check for the existence of attacks. Instead, we use our models and known attacks from previous works to check if the security properties proposed in the standard are enough to ensure the security of the protocol. Where they are not, we propose a new security property that could be added to the standard, encode it in TAMARIN, and use the tool to automatically show that it would be enough to stop a class of attacks, such as KRACK.

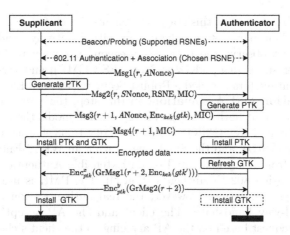

Fig. 1. IEEE 802.11 standard 4-way handshake and group key handshake

The main contributions of this work are:

- Presenting TAMARIN models of the 802.11 4-way handshake that exhibit several attacks [20, 22], and formally showing correctness of suggested fixes.
- Showing how to use TAMARIN to encode the security properties defined in the standard, in order to automatically check if the weaknesses that causes any attack violate any of these properties. We show that for the KRACK attacks they do not, indicating that the current list of security properties in the standard is insufficient.
- Proposing a set of new security properties to be added to the standard, and use TAMARIN to show how systems with this security property are not vulnerable to the attacks.

2   Preliminaries

The IEEE 802.11 Standard. This standard defines protocols for data confidentiality, mutual authentication, and key management, providing enhanced security at the medium access control (MAC) layer in wireless networks [3].

The original version of the standard [1] appeared in 1997, and defined the Wired Equivalent Privacy (WEP) security algorithm, based on the weak RC4 cipher. The vulnerable WEP was replaced with Wi-Fi Protected Access (WPA), as an intermediate measure, before the IEEE 802.11i amendment (WPA2) [2] was released in 2004. WPA includes the use of a message authentication code algorithm, coined as Message Integrity Check (MIC), as well as the TKIP cipher suite, which allows a more secure per-packet key system compared to the fixed key system used by WEP. The 802.11i amendment [2] and the current version of the standard [3] requires support of even more secure algorithm suites, discussed below. We summarise here the four stages of the 802.11 key generation process. We refer the reader to [3] for the full details.

- **Network Discovery.** In this stage, the clients search for available networks along with their parameters. Clients can either actively send and receive probes, or just observe the broadcast beacons passively to learn the supported cipher suites (e.g., TKIP and/or AES-CCMP), and version of WPA. This set of parameters is called a Robust Security Network Element (RSNE).
- **Authentication and Association.** In this step, the Pairwise Master Key (PMK) is derived at both ends. In WPA2-Personal mode, the PMK is derived using a Pre-Shared Key (PSK) with a length of 8 to 63 characters, the Service Set Identifier (SSID), and the SSID length, while in WPA2-Enterprise mode, it is derived from a key generated by an Extensible Authentication Protocol (EAP), e.g., using 802.1X authentication [4]. The PMK is used later in the temporal keys generation. However, the real authentication is carried out during the 4-way handshake. The client and the AP accept or reject the association request based on the AP agreeing to the client's choice of RSNE.
- **4-Way Handshake.** The 4-way handshake takes place to agree on a fresh session key, namely the Pairwise Transient Key (PTK), and optionally the Group Temporal Key (GTK); see Fig. 1. PTK derivation [3, Sec. 12.7.1.7.5] uses the shared PMK, a supplicant nonce S_{Nonce}, an authenticator nonce A_{Nonce}, and both MAC addresses. The PTK can be refreshed after a fixed time interval, or at request from either party, by executing another 4-way handshake. The PTK is split into a Key Confirmation Key (KCK), Key Encryption Key (KEK), and Temporal Key (TK). The KCK and KEK protect handshake messages, while the TK protects data frames through the data confidentiality protocol. The 4-way handshake also transports the current GTK to the supplicant. Every message in the 4-way handshake follows the layout of EAP over LAN Key frames (EAPOL-Key) [3], and we use Msg$n$ to denote the nth message in the handshake. The authenticator starts the handshake and increments the replay counter on every message sent. The supplicant replies to messages using the received replay counter.
- **Group Key Handshake.** The standard allows for refreshing the GTK regularly, using a group key handshake, to ensure that only active clients are in possession of it. This process is initiated by the authenticator sending group message 1, denoted GrMsg1, to all clients. The clients reply, in turn, with group message 2, GrMsg2, with the received replay counter; see Fig. 1.
- **Data Confidentiality and Integrity Support.** The standard defines several data confidentiality suites such as AES-CCMP and AES-GCMP as mandatory, but also TKIP for backwards interoperability with WPA [3]. All suites include message integrity of the data frames. For brevity, we use the same notation as in [22] to denote an encrypted frame $\mathrm{Enc}_k^n()$, being n the nonce (replay counter) in use, and k the key, i.e., PTK for unicast and GTK for broadcast messages.

We note that our focus is mainly on the attacks to the 4-way handshake. Therefore, the authentication and association stages are out of the scope of this paper, and we will hereafter assume that the PMK is already available at both ends.

Analysing Security Properties. The IEEE 802.11 standard lists five properties, labelled from a) to e), for the 4-way handshake [3, Sec. 12.6.14]. He *et al.* [14] aggregate four out of five of these security properties into *session authentication*, which can only be asserted when *key secrecy* is guaranteed. They formalise authentication in the cryptographic model using the notion of *matching conversations* [6], guaranteeing that the two entities have consistent views of the protocol runs. Using Protocol Composition Logic (PCL) [10], they verify that such properties hold. However, PCL has been subject of criticism by some authors such as [8], as it allows one to verify authentication protocols that rely on signing, but not those relying on decryption. More disconcertingly, there are no means to establish preceding actions in a thread. In contrast to matching conversations used in [14], we use standard notions of authentication from Lowe [17], e.g., mutual, injective agreement, to verify the security properties. Moreover, in their approach using PCL [14], the authors confirm that all their proofs were constructed manually. On the other hand, our verification using TAMARIN is among the first attempts to verify security properties of 802.11 automatically.

Concurrent to our work, Cremers *et al.* [9] have also developed a detailed TAMARIN model of the WPA2 protocol capable of detecting KRACK attacks, among others. Though yet to appear their work, as ours, verifies the effectiveness of the patched protocol, post-discovery of the KRACK attacks, in stopping all the attacks, including the KRACK attacks. However, our goals are different; our focus is on developing a framework to test the adequacy of the required security properties in spotting the attacks. Therefore, we only model the functionalities required to demonstrate the attacks (KRACK and downgrade), rather than the whole protocol.

The TAMARIN Prover and SAPiC. TAMARIN is a state-of-the-art tool for symbolic verification and automated analysis of security properties in protocols, under the Dolev-Yao model [11], with respect to an unbounded number of sessions. There are similar tools for symbolic verification, most notably ProVerif [7], where protocols are specified using applied pi-calculus [5]. In our approach, we have decided to implement our models with TAMARIN, since it can handle protocols with unrestricted global states and unbounded sessions. Sometimes, however, the user may have to provide auxiliary lemmas for complex protocols in order to help the tool terminate. Most importantly, TAMARIN has the *restriction* feature, which allows a property to be enforced on the traces. This feature is essential for our work, to verify if enforcing particular security properties would stop an attack. To the best of our knowledge, other tools such as ProVerif do not offer this feature and hence are not suitable to our approach.

More concretely, we have developed our models using the SAPiC front-end, which allows to specify TAMARIN models using processes. We provide a brief overview of these tools, but we refer the reader to [16,18] for further reference. SAPiC parses descriptions of protocols in an extension of the applied pi-calculus [5], called *stateful applied pi-calculus*, and converts them into *(labeled) multiset rewriting rules* (MSRs) to be analysed by TAMARIN.

$\langle P,Q \rangle ::=$		processes
	0	terminal (null) process
	$P \mid Q$	parallel composition of P and Q
	$!P$	replication of P
	$\nu\, a;\, P$	binds a to a new fresh value in P
	$\text{out}(m,t);\, P$	outputs message t on channel m
	$\text{in}\,(m,t);\, P$	inputs of message t on channel m
	if $Pred$ then P [else Q]	P if predicate $Pred$ holds; otherwise Q
	event F; P	executes event (action fact) F
	$P + Q$	non-deterministic choice
	insert $m,\, t;\, P$	inserts t at memory cell m
	delete $m;\, P$	deletes the content m
	lookup m as x in P [else Q]	if m exists, bind it to x in P; otw. Q
	lock $m;\, P$	gain exclusive access to cell m
	unlock $m;\, P$	waive exclusive access to m
	$[L]\, \text{-}\!\!\lvert A \rvert\!\!\rightarrow [R];\, P \quad (L,R,A \in \mathcal{F}^*)$	provides access to TAMARIN MSRs

Fig. 2. SAPiC syntax ($a \in FN$, $x \in \mathcal{V}$, $m,t \in \mathcal{T}$, $F \in \mathcal{F}$)

Figure 2 describes the SAPiC syntax. The calculus comprises an *order-sorted term algebra* with infinite sets of publicly known names PN, freshly generated names FN, and variables $\mathcal{V}$. It also comprises a signature Σ, i.e., a set of function symbols, each with an arity. The messages are elements of a set of terms $\mathcal{T}$ over PN, FN, and $\mathcal{V}$, built by applying the function symbols in Σ.

The set of facts is defined as $\mathcal{F} = \{F(t_1, \ldots, t_n) \mid t_i \in \mathcal{T}, F \in \Sigma \text{ of arity } k\}$. The special fact $K(m)$ states that the term m is known to the adversary. For a set of roles, the TAMARIN MSRs define how the system, i.e., protocol, can make a transition to a new state. An MSR is a triple of the form $[L]\,\text{-}\!\!\lvert A \rvert\!\!\rightarrow [R]$, where L and R are the premise and conclusion of the rule, respectively, and A is a set of action facts, modelled by SAPiC events. For a process P, its trace $\text{Tr}(P) = [F_1, \ldots, F_n]$ is an ordered sequence of action facts generated by firing the rules in order.

TAMARIN allows to express security properties as temporal, guarded first-order formulas, modelled as trace properties. The construct $F@i$ states the presence of the fact F at time point i. A property can be specified as a *lemma* to be tested if it holds or not, and enforced as a *restriction*, while testing the other lemmas in presence of this property [18].

3   Methodology for Analysing Security Properties

We summarise our process of analysing the security properties in Fig. 3. We start by building a model of a protocol with known attacks in Sect. 4. Subsequently, we verify all the security properties listed in the standard to see if they are satisfied or violated in Sect. 5. A violated security property can then be enforced as a restriction to check if it would stop the attacks, indicating an implementation issue. Alternatively, if all the security properties are verified, but the attack still exists, we can conclude that the security properties required by the standard are

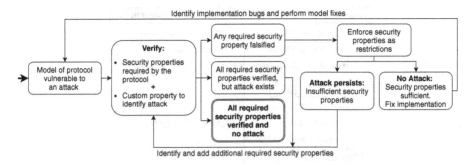

Fig. 3. Flow diagram for verifying security properties, identifying new ones, and fixing the model against an attack

insufficient and need to be augmented. After analysing the attacks, we propose a security property corresponding to the attack, shown below in Sect. 6. To test that the new property is successful in stopping the attack, we first place it as a lemma in the model and expect it to be falsified. Then, we enforce this property as a restriction in the model, expecting that it stops the attack. This helps us to verify if the attack corresponds to the new proposed security property. Finally, we execute the protocol model after fixing the vulnerability, to verify the absence of the attack. The verification of our newly proposed security properties and the fixes proves both the adequacy of the final set of properties, and correctness of the fixes in the protocol. We discuss this in Sects. 6 and 7.

4 Formal Models of the 802.11 4-Way Handshake Attacks

We present some variants of the KRACK attacks, exploiting nonce reuse [22], and a downgrade attack from [20]. Along with the attack steps, we also highlight some relevant details of our SAPiC models for the attacks and for the security lemmas corresponding to each one. Some of the details, e.g., MIC, the usage of cipher suites in encryption, or some events are omitted here due to space constraints, but they can be easily understood from the context. The complete source for the models and mechanised proofs are available at [19].

4.1 KRACK Attacks

The KRACK attacks exploit vulnerabilities in the 802.11 key management protocols [22]. An adversary tricks a victim into reinstalling an already used key by dropping, delaying or altering the order of the 4-way handshake messages between two honest principals. On every key installation, the standard mandates that the replay counter (nonce) of the data confidentiality protocol be reset. The adversary can collect different encrypted messages using the same key and nonce: messages sent after the initial key installation, and messages sent after the key reinstallation. The adversary can then use this information to attack the data confidentiality protocol. The practical implications of the attack may enable the

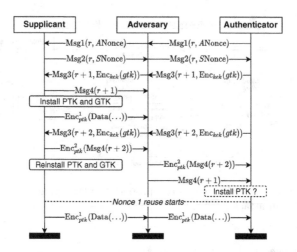

Fig. 4. KRACK - plaintext retransmission of message 3 after PTK install

adversary to replay, decrypt or even forge the data packets, depending on the choice of the cipher suite (e.g., TKIP, AES-CCMP,AES-GCMP). We refer the reader to [15, 22] for the detailed consequences of the attack.

The underlying causes of the attacks are the unclear standard specifications, such as the authenticator accepting any replay counter previously used in the 4-way handshake, not only the latest one [3, Sec. 12.7.6.5]. However, in practice, many APs fail to validate it, and imprudently accept an older replay counter.

We have successfully modelled several KRACK attacks exploiting the retransmission of message 3 and forcing nonce reuse [22]. We remark that the goal of our models is not to verify the compromise of the data confidentiality protocol. Instead, we aim at detecting the sufficient conditions that allow an adversary to exploit it, i.e., reinstallations of the same key.

Retransmission of Message 3 After PTK Install. This variant of KRACK [22, Sec. 3.3] occurs when the supplicant accepts plaintext retransmission of message 3, even after a PTK has been installed. The message flow of the attack is shown in Fig. 4, and the outline of our model of the supplicant and authenticator are in Fig. 5. Note that we prepend 'S_' and 'A_' to the events executed at the supplicant and authenticator, respectively. The main process is defined as $\nu\ pmk$; (!Supplicant | Authenticator), instantiating an arbitrary number of supplicant processes. Our model computes the PTK [3, Sec. 12.7.1.7.5] with the identifiers A_{id}, S_{id} acting as the MAC addresses as follows:

$$ptk = \mathrm{CalcPtk}(pmk, A_{\mathrm{Nonce}}, S_{\mathrm{Nonce}}, A_{\mathrm{id}}, S_{\mathrm{id}}).$$

The adversary sits between the supplicant and the authenticator to perform a man-in-the-middle (MitM) attack, and forwards messages 1–3 normally. The event S_InstallsPtk(S_{id}, ptk) captures an initial PTK install, after which the

Supplicant :=
ν S_{id}; out(S_{id});
!(in(A_{id});
  in(Msg1(r, A_{Nonce}));
  ν S_{Nonce};
  let ptk = CalcPtk(pmk, A_{Nonce}, ...) in
  out(Msg2(r, S_{Nonce}));
  in(Msg3($r + 1$, A_{Nonce}, $\text{Enc}_{kek}(gtk)$));
  event Running(S_{id}, A_{id}, $pars$);
  out(Msg4($r + 1$));
  event S_InstallsPtk(S_{id}, ptk);
  event S_InstallsGtk(S_{id}, gtk);
  ((event Commit(S_{id}, A_{id}, $pars$)
) +
  (in(Msg3($r + 2$, A_{Nonce}, $\text{Enc}_{kek}(gtk)$));
    event Running(S_{id}, A_{id}, $pars$);
    out(Enc_{ptk}(Msg4($r + 2$)));
    event S_InstallsPtk(S_{id}, ptk);
    event S_InstallsGtk(S_{id}, gtk);
    event Commit(S_{id}, A_{id}, $pars$)
)))

Authenticator :=
ν A_{id}; out(A_{id});
!(in(S_{id});
  ν r;
  ν A_{Nonce};
  out(Msg1(r, A_{Nonce}));
  let ptk = CalcPtk(pmk, ...) in
  in(Msg2(r, S_{Nonce}));
  ν gtk;
  event Running(A_{id}, S_{id}, $pars$);
  event A_InstallsGtk(gtk);
  out(Msg3($r + 1$, A_{Nonce}, $\text{Enc}_{kek}(gtk)$));
  ((in(Msg4($r + 1$));
    event A_InstallsPtk(ptk);
    event Commit(A_{id}, S_{id}, $pars$)
) +
  (out(Msg3($r + 2$, A_{Nonce}, ...)));
    in(Enc_{ptk}(Msg4($r + 2$)));
    event A_InstallsPtk(ptk);
    event Commit(A_{id}, S_{id}, $pars$)
)))

Fig. 5. Model outline for supplicant and authenticator vulnerable to KRACK attack based on plaintext retransmission of message 3

supplicant can send encrypted frames using the encryption key TK associated to PTK. Message 4 is blocked from reaching the authenticator by the adversary. The model uses the non-deterministic choice in the authenticator process via the + operator from the SAPiC calculus. Therefore, it captures either the reception of message 4, and installs the PTK, or timeouts and retransmits message 3 with an updated replay counter, and waits again for the confirmation.

Similarly, in order to capture the fact that the state machine of the supplicant accepts plaintext retransmission of message 3, we also branch the supplicant process, in order to capture traces completing a normal run of the protocol, and traces with an adversary blocking message 4. This latter case matches the attack scenario with the supplicant reinstalling an already in-use PTK (and GTK). It follows that the next data frames sent by the supplicant will be encrypted with a reused nonce. Our model, therefore, is aimed at capturing the traces with key reinstallations on the supplicant side using the same PTK already installed.

Retransmission of Message 3 Before PTK Install. This KRACK attack has two variants with the supplicant accepting either a plaintext or encrypted retransmission of message 3 with the PTK yet to be installed [22, Sec. 3.4].

The first case is shown in Fig. 6. This attack assumes that the authenticator performs its actions as expected. The first two messages are transmitted normally. However, the original message 3 is blocked by the adversary while he waits for retransmitted of message 3. Both messages are then forwarded to the supplicant. This triggers a race condition between the CPU and the network

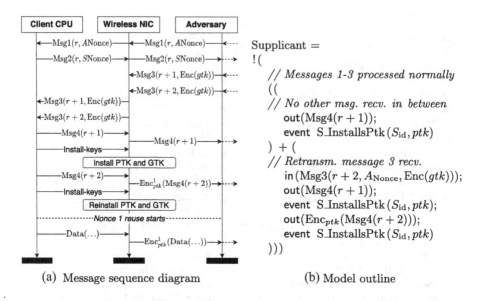

(a) Message sequence diagram   (b) Model outline

Fig. 6. KRACK - plaintext retransmission of message 3 before PTK install

interface controller (NIC), which causes that the same key be reinstalled. In our model for this attack, Fig. 6b, the supplicant comprises both the NIC and the CPU, and it considers two branches in order to capture an implementation vulnerable to the attack: one where the 4-way handshake follows the normal course, and another where the attacker is able to cause key reinstallation.

The second case of this attack is presented in Fig. 7. The main difference is that it can only be executed during the PTK rekey phase. After an initial successful handshake, both principals install a PTK. During the PTK rekey process, the adversary follows the same strategy as above: it waits for a retransmission of message 3. This time, the messages are encrypted under the installed PTK, but the adversary is able to identify what particular message is being sent (e.g., by timeouts or message lengths). By appropriately delaying and forwarding the messages, the adversary causes a reinstall of the PTK being refreshed, ptk'. Our model (Fig. 7b) captures an arbitrary number of PTK rekey negotiations, and, again, it branches non-deterministically to capture the transitions of a supplicant state machine vulnerable to the attack.

For all three cases above (Figs. 4, 6 and 7), we query for the absence of KRACK attacks with lemma: "given an installation of PTK by the supplicant, it is not the case that there exists an earlier installation with the same PTK,"

$$\forall id, ptk, t_1. \ \text{S\_InstallsPtk}(id, ptk)@t_1 \Rightarrow$$
$$\neg(\exists t_2. \ \text{S\_InstallsPtk}(id, ptk)@t_2 \wedge (t_2 < t_1)). \quad \text{(NoKrackPtk)}$$

The events S_InstallsPtk are placed in the parts of the model where the primitive MLME-SETKEYS.request [3] is called, which causes nonce reset.

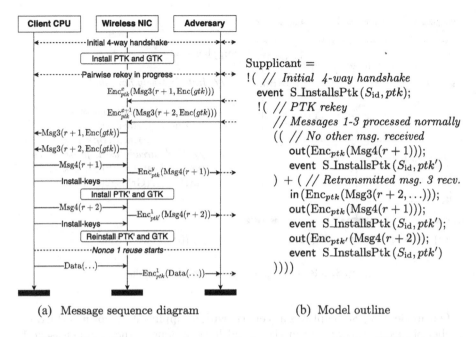

(a) Message sequence diagram   (b) Model outline

Fig. 7. KRACK - encrypted retransmission of message 3 before PTK install

As expected, our TAMARIN models [19] falsify Lemma (NoKrackPtk), proving the existence of KRACK, allowing an adversary to cause key reinstall, nonce reuse and break the security guarantees of the data confidentiality protocol.

Attack Against the Group Key Handshake. This variant of the KRACK attack targets the group key handshake, and tricks the supplicant into reinstalling a GTK, rather than a PTK [22, Sec. 4.1]. The attack is shown in Fig. 8. Note that the group key handshake runs encrypted by the already installed PTK. The standard requires that the supplicant install the GTK upon receipt of group message 1, regardless of whether it is a retransmission or not, and reply with group message 2. The adversary delays group message 2 from reaching the authenticator, triggering retransmission of group message 1. Now, the adversary forwards both versions of group message 1 to the supplicant, which causes a GTK install and subsequent reinstall. This will allow the attacker to replay group data frames to the supplicant [22].

To capture the reinstall of the GTK, TAMARIN falsifies the following lemma stating that "given an installation of GTK by the supplicant, it is not the case that there exists an earlier installation with the same GTK,"

$$\forall id, gtk, t_1.\ \text{S\_InstallsGtk}(id, gtk)@t_1 \Rightarrow$$
$$\neg(\exists t_2.\ \text{S\_InstallsGtk}(id, gtk)@t_2 \wedge (t_2 < t_1)). \quad \text{(NoKrackGtk)}$$

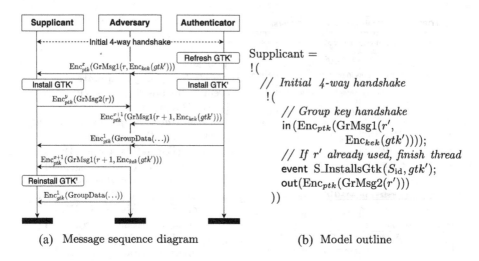

(a) Message sequence diagram   (b) Model outline

Fig. 8. KRACK against group key handshake

Our model (Fig. 8b) captures a scenario with a supplicant accepting arbitrary number of executions of the group key handshake, as long as the group message 1 has an increased replay counter. We note that for this model we assume an initial valid 4-way handshake without exhibiting PTK reinstall.

4.2   Cipher Suite Downgrade

The downgrade attack we consider [20] is limited to the authenticator-side only. In a correct implementation, a client should be able to detect this attack easily by observing inconsistencies in the RSNE information. Recall from Sect. 2 that the RSNE information is selected in the association stage in plaintext, and subsequently encrypted and transmitted as part of message 3, as shown in Fig. 1. The supplicant must verify that the RSNE information observed in the association stage matches with the authenticated contents of message 3, and it should terminate the handshake otherwise.

In a downgrade attack, depicted in Fig. 9, the adversary forces GTK encryption with a weak cipher suite (RC4), rather than the intended strong cipher suite (AES-CCMP). The attack was discovered on the access point TP-Link WP841P [20, Sec. 5.2]. The authenticator advertises support for AES-CCMP during the association stage. However, it will follow the supplicant in switching the cipher suite in mid-handshake process, accepting the TKIP-based message 2.

An adversary acts as a MitM by negotiating the AES-CCMP suite with the authenticator, and TKIP with the supplicant, as message 1 is in plain. The supplicant calculates the PTK and replies with message 2 using the TKIP suite. The authenticator accepts the message, overrides its initial AES-CCMP selection, and responds with a well-formed TKIP message 3 containing the GTK encrypted with RC4. The adversary can now exploit the weakness of this cipher

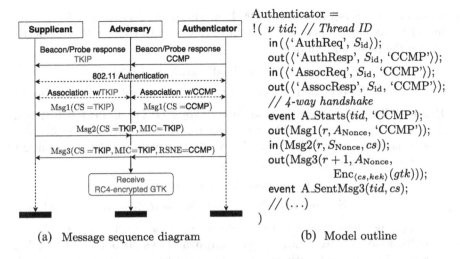

(a) Message sequence diagram   (b) Model outline

Fig. 9. Downgrade Attack on 802.11 (TP-Link WP841P)

to recover the GTK [21]. The RSNE mismatch can be easily detected on forwarding of message 3 to the supplicant, which can drop the connection. Unfortunately, by this time, the adversary is already in possession of the RC4-encrypted GTK.

Encryption with different cipher suites can be modelled, e.g., with a signature Enc$'$, Dec$'$ indicating the cipher suite cs as an additional parameter. Then,

$$\forall m, k, cs. \ \text{Dec}'_k(\text{Enc}'_k(m, cs), cs) = m.$$

Note, that this theory is semantically equivalent to the usual symmetric encryption using as key the tuple $k' = \langle cs, k \rangle$, because $\text{Dec}_{\langle cs,k \rangle}(\text{Enc}_{\langle cs,k \rangle}(m)) = m$.

Our TAMARIN model queries that "for each run of the protocol, the cipher suites used by them will be the same," implying that a change of the cipher suite in between a run is impossible. As expected, the lemma below is falsified:

$$\forall tid, cs_1, cs_2, t_1, t_2. \ \text{A\_SentMsg3}(tid, cs_1)@t_1 \wedge$$
$$\text{A\_Starts}(tid, cs_2)@t_2 \Rightarrow (cs_1 = cs_2). \qquad \text{(NoDowngrade)}$$

5 Analysis of IEEE 802.11 Security Properties

In this section, we list the five properties a)-e) specified for the 4-way handshake in the 802.11 standard [3, Sec. 12.6.14]. These properties overlap with each other and cannot be easily encoded into conventional queries, e.g., secrecy or authentication. Therefore, we sometimes define multiple security lemmas that jointly satisfy a given property. Moreover, the standard is unclear about what properties are satisfied by the group key handshake. In that case, we consider an extension of property c) below for GTK. We recall that we prepend 'S_' and 'A_' to the supplicant and authenticator events, respectively.

a) **Confirm the existence of the PMK at the peer.** As stated in Sect. 2, our model treats this property as a premise. However, to confirm this property, we use the following lemma:

$$\forall id_1, id_2, pmk_1, pmk_2, t_1, t_2.\ \text{A\_HasPmk}(id_1, pmk_1)@t_1 \wedge$$
$$\text{S\_HasPmk}(id_2, pmk_2)@t_2 \Rightarrow (pmk_1 = pmk_2). \qquad \text{(ConfPmk)}$$

b) **Ensure that the security association keys (PTK/GTK) are fresh.** This security property states that at every run (thread tid) of the protocol it must generate a fresh PTK/GTK. We verify this property at the supplicant side through lemma

$$\forall id_1, id_2, ptk, t_1, t_2.\ \text{S\_ComputesPtk}(id_1, ptk)@t_1 \wedge$$
$$\text{S\_ComputesPtk}(id_2, ptk)@t_2 \Rightarrow (tid_1 = tid_2). \qquad \text{(FreshPtk)}$$

Similarly, we define Lemma (FreshGtk) for the case of GTK (omitted).

c) **Synchronise the installation of temporal keys into the MAC.** We consider the strongest authentication property from Lowe's hierarchy [17], namely, injective *agreement*. For the case of PTK, we verify that: "for each S_CommitPtk event executed by the supplicant S_{id}, the associated authenticator A_{id} executed the corresponding A_RunningPtk earlier, and for each run of the protocol there is a unique S_CommitPtk for each A_RunningPtk,"

$$\forall S_{id}, A_{id}, pars, t_1.\ \text{S\_CommitPtk}(S_{id}, A_{id}, pars)@t_1 \Rightarrow$$
$$((\exists t_2.\ \text{A\_RunningPtk}(A_{id}, S_{id}, pars)@t_2 \wedge (t_2 < t_1))$$
$$\wedge \neg(\exists S'_{id}, A'_{id}, t_3.\ \text{S\_CommitPtk}(S'_{id}, A'_{id}, pars)@t_3 \wedge \neg(t_3 = t_1))). $$
$$\text{(AgreePtk)}$$

Obviously, the set of parameters *pars* must contain the value of the PTK. S_CommitPtk events are placed as late as possible on the supplicant side. A_RunningPtk events are executed as earlier as possible, when all the parameters to agree are available to the authenticator. In order to capture mutual agreement, the lemma also needs to include the case when the roles of the authenticator and supplicant are reversed. For brevity, we omit this case in our exposition, but it can be found in the source of our models [19].

As customary, authentication requires key secrecy to be asserted. We verify this using the following lemma for PTK:

$$\forall id, ptk, t_1.\ \text{S\_InstallsPtk}(id, ptk)@t_1 \Rightarrow \neg(\exists t_2.\ K(ptk)@t_2). \qquad \text{(SecretPtk)}$$

Again, S_InstallsPtk models the primitive MLME-SETKEYS.request [3], and we require that any installed PTK is unknown to the adversary.

For GTK, we define the Lemmas (AgreeGtk) and (SecretGtk) equivalently. Moreover, we also need to capture *weak agreement* [17] of GTK in the group key handshake, through the lemma

$$\forall S_{id}, A_{id}, pars, t_1.\ \text{S\_WCommitGtk}(S_{id}, A_{id}, pars)@t_1 \Rightarrow$$
$$((\exists t_2.\ \text{A\_WRunningGtk}(A_{id}, S_{id}, pars)@t_2 \wedge (t_2 < t_1)),$$
$$\text{(WeakAgreeGtk)}$$

Table 1. TAMARIN results of testing properties a)–e) from the 802.11 standard and proposed property f) in Sect. 5. *No[Attack]* refers to (NoKrackPtk), (NoKrackGtk) or (NoDowngrade) accordingly. (✓ verified; ✗ falsified; – n/a)

Lemmas	No[Attack]	(ConfPmk)	(FreshPtk)	(FreshGtk)	(AgreePtk)	(AgreeGtk)	(WeakAgreeGtk)	(SecretPtk)	(SecretGtk)	(SameGtk)	(AgreeCs)	(NoPtkReuse)	(NoGtkReuse)
	–	a) ConfPmk	b) FreshKeys		c) SynchronisedKeys					d) SameGTK	e) ConfCiphers	f) NoKeyReuse	
PTK reinst. Figs. 4, 5	✗	✓	✓	✓	✓	✓	–	✓	✓	✓	✓	✗	✗
PTK reinst. Fig. 7	✗	✓	✓	✓	✓	✓	–	✓	✓	✓	✓	✗	✗
PTK reinst. Fig. 9	✗	✓	✓	✓	✓	✓	–	✓	✓	✓	✓	✗	✗
GTK reinst. Fig. 11	✗	✓	✓	✓	✓	✓	–	✓	✓	✓	✓	–	✗
Downgrade Fig. 13	✗	✓	✓	✓	✓	✓	–	✓	✓	✓	✗	✓	✓

which includes the GTK in *pars*. As opposed to (AgreeGtk) in the 4-way handshake, the agreement in the group key handshake is not injective, because multiple retransmissions of the same GTK are allowed.

d) **Transfer the GTK from the Authenticator to the Supplicant.** We verify if the GTK received by the supplicant is the same GTK calculated and forwarded by the authenticator using lemma

$$\forall id, gtk, t_1. \; S\_InstallsGtk(id, gtk)@t_1 \Rightarrow$$
$$(\exists t_2. \; A\_GeneratesGtk(gtk)@t_2 \wedge (t_2 < t_1)). \qquad \text{(SameGtk)}$$

e) **Confirm the selection of cipher suites.** We capture injective agreement of the cipher suite with Lemma (AgreeCs), similar to (AgreePtk) above, by using the cipher suite within the parameters *pars*.

We queried the lemmas defined for the above five properties in the TAMARIN models presented in Sect. 4, in order to verify them in presence of KRACK and downgrade attacks. Unexpectedly, all of the lemmas were reported as verified when KRACK attacks were present, as shown in Table 1. In the case of the downgrade attack, however, TAMARIN reported expected violation of Lemma (AgreeCs) only.

6 Proposing New Security Properties

Security Property for KRACK Attack. Section 5 clearly establishes the inadequacy of set of security properties mandated by the IEEE 802.11 standard to capture security violation by KRACK attacks reviewed in Sect. 4. Though IEEE has since addressed the issue of nonce reuse in 802.11 implementations [12], and the Wi-Fi Alliance tests the devices before certifying them for WPA2/3 [23], there is no mention of security properties being added to the standard that could capture various KRACK variants such as the ones presented by

Lemmas (NoKrackPtk) and (NoKrackGtk). Accordingly, we propose an additional security property to capture such vulnerabilities:

f) Ensure that the security association keys are not used more than once.

The security property f) is encoded, using the following lemma, in TAMARIN. All the KRACK attack models from Sect. 4 violate either one or both properties (See Table 1), i.e., the KRACK attacks are now captured by property f):

$$\forall id, ptk, t_1, t_2.\ \text{S\_InstallsPtk}(id, ptk)@t_1 \land$$
$$\text{S\_InstallsPtk}(id, ptk)@t_2 \Rightarrow (t_1 = t_2). \qquad \text{(NoPtkReuse)}$$

Equivalently, we define the Lemma (NoGtkReuse) using GTK in place of PTK.

Security Property for Downgrade Attack. The downgrade attack from Fig. 9 violates property e) through the Lemma (AgreeCs). Surprisingly, the attack continue to exist even after enforcing this property as restriction. Since enforcing the agreement property on cipher suite does not stop the attack, it is violating a property not present in the standard. A detailed analysis of property e) along with the downgrade attack suggests that though the standard guarantees authentication w.r.t. other party, it does not perform agreement with itself. Accordingly, we suggest the following additional security property g), as Lemma (ValidCipherSuite), to the model of Fig. 9b that captures this attack (results omitted from Table 1 due to space constraints).

g) The cipher suite that the authenticator started with is the cipher suite that the authenticator finishes with, and is the strongest one from the available choices.

As expected, the downgrade attack from Sect. 4 is captured by property g), which is encoded in TAMARIN using lemma

$$\forall tid, cs_1, cs_2, t_1, t_2.\ \text{A\_SentMsg3}(tid, cs_1)@t_1 \land$$
$$\text{A\_Starts}(tid, cs_2)@t_2 \Rightarrow (cs_1 = cs_2). \qquad \text{(ValidCipherSuite)}$$

To verify that our proposed security properties f) and g) correspond to respective attacks, we fix the respective TAMARIN models of Sect. 4 by enforcing (NoPtkReuse), (NoGtkReuse) and (ValidCipherSuite) as *restrictions*.

On testing the security properties from Sect. 4, i.e., Lemmas (NoKrackPtk), (NoKrackGtk), and (NoDowngrade), TAMARIN verifies them in the fixed model, proving that the proposed security properties are successful in stopping these attacks.

7   Verifying the Mitigations to the Models

Finally, we fix the KRACK models, from Sect. 4, making sure that they follow the newly proposed security property f), i.e., disconnect if there is an attempt to install with the same PTK or GTK, and then execute the model again. After the fix, both of the attack lemmas, i.e., Lemmas (NoKrackPtk) and (NoKrackGtk), along with the security properties (NoPtkReuse) and (NoGtkReuse) are verified. The absence of the attack, with the new security properties verified, shows the validity of the proposed fix. This result is also a verification of the proposed countermeasure for KRACK by [22].

Similarly, the downgrade attack from Fig. 9 can be easily detected at the supplicant side [20], and can be stopped if the authenticator implementation disallows the change of cipher suites mid-handshake. Accordingly, we fix the model ensuring that it rejects a connection where the authenticator does not start and finish with the same cipher suite. After fixing it, TAMARIN reports the attack Lemma (NoDowngrade) as verified, i.e., the downgrade attack no longer exists, and that the mitigation is valid. Both the fixed TAMARIN models, of KRACK and downgrade attacks, are publicly available at [19].

8   Conclusion and Further Work

We have presented formal models of various KRACK attacks on the IEEE 802.11 4-way handshake and group key handshake, and downgrade attacks on implementations of the 4-way handshake. Using the automatic verification tool TAMARIN, we verify all the security properties of the 4-way handshake mandated by the 802.11 standard, in the presence of KRACK and downgrade vulnerabilities. We find that KRACK attacks do not violate any of the required security properties. We conclude that the set of properties is inadequate to capture these attacks. Using a novel approach, we propose additional security properties to be added to the 802.11 standard, enabling it to capture them. We also demonstrate that enforcing these security properties in our model successfully stops these attacks. Accordingly, we fix the models with countermeasures to mitigate the attacks and verify all the security properties, providing a formal proof of correctness of the recommended countermeasures. Our novel technique can strengthen protocol specifications, by testing the adequacy of the set of required security properties against known or newly discovered attacks, and by augmenting them with new properties, if required. For future work, we would like to extend it to other use cases, i.e., to test the set of required security properties for other protocols against known attacks on them.

Acknowledgements. We would like to thank Robert Künnemann, Chris McMahon Stone and Mathy Vanhoef for useful discussions. We would also like to thank the anonymous reviewers for their insightful comments and suggestions. This work was partially supported by the European Union's Horizon 2020 research and innovation programme under grant agreement No. 779391 (FutureTPM).

References

1. IEEE Standard for Wireless LAN Medium Access Control (MAC) and Physical Layer (PHY) specifications. IEEE Std. 802.11-1997, November 1997

2. Wireless LAN Medium Access Control (MAC) and Physical Layer (PHY) Specifications: Amendment 6. IEEE Std. 802.11i-2004, July 2004
3. Wireless LAN Medium Access Control (MAC) and Physical Layer (PHY) specifications. IEEE Std. 802.11-2016, December 2016
4. IEEE Standard for Local and Metropolitan Area Networks-Port-Based Network Access Control. IEEE Std. 802.1X-2020, February 2020
5. Abadi, M., Fournet, C.: Mobile values, new names, and secure communication. ACM SIGPLAN Not. **36**(3), 104–115 (2001)
6. Bellare, M., Rogaway, P.: Entity authentication and key distribution. In: Stinson, D.R. (ed.) CRYPTO 1993. LNCS, vol. 773, pp. 232–249. Springer, Heidelberg (1994). https://doi.org/10.1007/3-540-48329-2_21
7. Blanchet, B., Smyth, B., Cheval, V., Sylvestre, M.: ProVerif 2.02: Automatic Cryptographic Protocol Verifier, User Manual and Tutorial, July 2020
8. Cremers, C.: On the protocol composition logic PCL. In: ACM Symposium on Information, Computer and Communications Security (ASIACCS), Tokyo, Japan, pp. 66–76, March 2008
9. Cremers, C., Kiesl, B., Medinger, N.: A formal analysis of IEEE 802.11's WPA2: countering the kracks caused by cracking the counters. In: Proceedings of the USENIX Security Symposium (USENIX Security), pp. 1–17. Virtual Event, August 2020 (to appear)
10. Datta, A., Derek, A., Mitchell, J.C., Roy, A.: Protocol composition logic (PCL). Electron. Notes Theor. Comput. Sci. **172**, 311–358 (2007)
11. Dolev, D., Yao, A.: On the security of public key protocols. IEEE Trans. Inf. Theory **29**(2), 198–208 (1983)
12. Harkins, D., Malinen, J.: Addressing the issue of nonce reuse in 802.11 implementations, October 2017. https://mentor.ieee.org/802.11/dcn/17/11-17-1602-03-000m-nonce-reuse-prevention.docx
13. He, C., Mitchell, J.C.: Analysis of the 802.11i 4-way handshake. In: Proceedings of the ACM Workshop on Wireless Security (WiSe), Philadelphia, PA, pp. 43–50, October 2004
14. He, C., Sundararajan, M., Datta, A., Derek, A., Mitchell, J.C.: A modular correctness proof of IEEE 802.11i and TLS. In: ACM Conference on Computer and Communications Security (CCS), Alexandria, VA, pp. 2–15, November 2005
15. Joux, A.: Authentication failures in NIST version of GCM. Pub. C. to NIST (2006)
16. Kremer, S., Künnemann, R.: Automated analysis of security protocols with global state. J. Comput. Secur. **24**(5), 583–616 (2016)
17. Lowe, G.: A hierarchy of authentication specifications. In: Proceedings of the IEEE Computer Security Foundations Workshop (CSFW), Rockport, MA, pp. 31–43, June 1997
18. Meier, S., Schmidt, B., Cremers, C., Basin, D.: The TAMARIN prover for the symbolic analysis of security protocols. In: Sharygina, N., Veith, H. (eds.) CAV 2013. LNCS, vol. 8044, pp. 696–701. Springer, Heidelberg (2013). https://doi.org/10.1007/978-3-642-39799-8_48
19. Singh, R.R., Moreira, J., Chothia, T., Ryan, M.D.: TAMARIN prover models of attacks on the 802.11 4-way handshake to verify security properties (source code and proofs) (2020). http://people.du.ac.in/~rrsingh/wpa2models
20. McMahon Stone, C., Chothia, T., de Ruiter, J.: Extending automated protocol state learning for the 802.11 4-way handshake. In: Lopez, J., Zhou, J., Soriano, M. (eds.) ESORICS 2018. LNCS, vol. 11098, pp. 325–345. Springer, Cham (2018). https://doi.org/10.1007/978-3-319-99073-6_16

21. Vanhoef, M., Piessens, F.: Predicting, decrypting, and abusing WPA2/802.11 group keys. In: Proceedings of the USENIX Security Symposium, pp. 673–688 (2016)
22. Vanhoef, M., Piessens, F.: Key reinstallation attacks: forcing nonce reuse in WPA2. In: Proceedings of the ACM Conference on Computer and Communications Security (CSS), Dallas, TX, pp. 1313–1328 (2017)
23. Wi-Fi Alliance: Security update october 2017, October 2017. https://www.wi-fi.org/security-update-october-2017

Reducing the Forensic Footprint with Android Accessibility Attacks

Yonas Leguesse[1]([⊠]) , Mark Vella[1] , Christian Colombo[1] ,
and Julio Hernandez-Castro[2]

[1] Department of Computer Science, University of Malta, Msida, Malta
{yonas.leguesse.05,mark.vella,christian.colombo}@um.edu.mt
[2] School of Computing, Cornwallis South, University of Kent, Canterbury, UK
jch27@kent.ac.uk

Abstract. Android accessibility features include a robust set of tools allowing developers to create apps for assisting people with disabilities. Unfortunately, this useful set of tools can also be abused and turned into an attack vector, providing malware with the ability to interact and read content from third-party apps.

In this work, we are the first to study the impact that the stealthy exploitation of Android accessibility services can have on significantly reducing the forensic footprint of malware attacks, thus hindering both live and post-incident forensic investigations. We show that through Living off the Land (LotL) tactics, or by offering a malware-only substitute for attacks typically requiring more elaborate schemes, accessibility-based malware can be rendered virtually undetectable.

In the LotL approach, we demonstrate accessibility-enabled SMS and command and control (C2) capabilities. As for the latter, we show a complete cryptocurrency wallet theft, whereby the accessibility trojan can hijack the entire withdrawal process of a widely used app, including two-factor authentication (2FA). In both cases, we demonstrate how the attacks result in significantly diminished forensic evidence when compared to similar attacks not employing accessibility tools, even to the extent of maintaining device take-over without requiring malware persistence.

Keywords: Android security · Android accessibility attacks ·
Anti-forensics · Malware detection

1 Introduction

Mobile devices have evolved significantly, both in sophistication and market adoption, over the last decade. In 2019, Google announced that there were over 2.5 billion active Android devices [1], turning it into the largest operating system in terms of existing users. From a cybercriminal's perspective, this constitutes a large and attractive target. Indeed, the increase in mobile device usage has resulted in a steady rise in mobile malware over recent years [2].

© The Author(s) 2020
K. Markantonakis and M. Petrocchi (Eds.): STM 2020, LNCS 12386, pp. 22–38, 2020.
https://doi.org/10.1007/978-3-030-59817-4_2

Moreover, financial services such as banking and cryptocurrency exchanges are firmly moving towards mobile platforms, turning Android devices into an appealing and potentially very profitable target. Malware detection on Android devices follows a typical multi-stage approach, aiming for early detection and removal. Google relies on automated malware analysis [3] to scan all apps uploaded to their app store. This is complemented by on-device scans, where additional information related to the actual operational environment becomes available. Besides this, the user is continuously prompted by applications requesting sensitive permissions or engaging in potentially dangerous operations [4], both aimed at quickly detecting, exposing and stopping app misdemeanour.

However, at times stealthy malware does still make it through all these protective layers, ultimately getting exposed during later infection stages through indicators of compromise such as expensive mobile service bills or a severely reduced battery life. At this point, and incident response investigation will try to trace attack activity back to the enabler malware artefacts [5] and take the necessary rectification steps. While current malware already uses a combination of emulation detection [6], code obfuscation and social engineering tricks [7] for evading detection, we argue that the addition of lesser-known accessibility services can significantly hamper malware detection and investigation.

The abuse of accessibility services can result in a significant reduction in the number of malware-specific components, which can, in some cases, not be necessary at all even while the device remains under full control of the attacker. The net result is that the number of forensic artefacts or the overall forensic footprint, heavily relied upon by on-device malware detectors and incident response tools is vastly reduced. It is also possible to not only diminish but also to manipulate this footprint so that the artefacts left become misleading, so that the true origins, causes and perpetrators of the attack remaining elusive.

Typical sources of forensic artefacts include the suspicious binary itself, probes and logs generated during its execution, and memory artefacts left during and after execution [8], to mention only a few. For example, when looking for an SMS-sending malware, a detection/response tool may look for the SMS-sending code within the app's decompiled resources, as well as for the artefacts left after the execution of the SMS-sending functionality. Android performs in the background a sequence of events that allow for the SMS sending to take place. These include data repository insertions, inter-app communications, and radio communications. Remnants from all these activities could expose the malware and therefore constitute valuable forensic artefacts. Any malware that attempts to reduce this forensic footprint will, at the same time, benefit from a reduced chance of detection.

In this work, we demonstrate that the deliberate misuse of the Android accessibility service offers one such possible method of evasion. While initially conceived to render all Android apps automatically accessible to all end-users, this feature ended up being abused by app developers for all sorts of inter-app communication [9], e.g. password managers. Eventually, malware authors aiming to bypass Android's security model also caught up with this feature. Since all previous efforts to remove re-purposed accessibility apps or to render accessibility safer have proven unsuccessful, accessibility has now become the Achilles heel [10] of Android's security. The misuse of accessibility services is increasingly becoming a staple of Android malware, ranging from banking trojans, e.g. Gustuff [11] and EventBot [12], to fully-fledged malware bots, e.g. Cerberus [11] and DEFENSOR ID [10].

While previous work primarily focuses on the dangers of accessibility in terms of malicious capabilities, in this paper we study for the first time the increased stealth features of this attack strategy. We show that through Living off the Land (LotL) tactics, which is already very popular in Windows malware [13], accessibility malware can be rendered virtually undetectable, even by state-of-the-art detection and recovery tools.

Our study confirms that accessibility attacks can significantly reduce the forensic footprint when compared to more standard, non-accessibility attacks. Specifically, we make use of a proof-of-concept malware that abuses SMS functionality and breaks the two-factor authentication (2FA) of a widely used cryptowallet app. We are able to demonstrate a significantly reduced forensic footprint in the sources of evidence used by current malware detection and incident response tools. In summary, we make the following contributions:

- We demonstrate that through the abuse of the accessibility service, LotL tactics can be performed on Android (Subsects. 3.1–3.4).
- We then describe a novel way to implement a cryptocurrency wallet theft. The accessibility malware hijacks the entire withdrawal process, including 2FA authentication, thus providing a malware-only alternative to more elaborate cybercrime schemes.
- This averts forensic evidence on other channels (Subsect. 3.5). Our research confirms that accessibility attacks significantly reduce the forensic footprint when compared to non-accessibility attacks (Sect. 4).

2   Background

2.1   Android Attack Vectors

Android malware typically consists of packed or embedded malicious code inside seemingly or truly benign applications. The malicious code then performs malign operations on the victim's device by executing a series of commands either hard-coded or received through the command and control (C2) channel [14]. However, if this code requires the use of OS features deemed as dangerous, it must request the appropriate permission or functionality. Examples of these are the SEND_SMS permission, or access to the camera. At this moment, malware must somehow trick the victim into enabling the relevant permission.

A more advanced vector, known as capability leak, involves abusing privileged components in third-party apps that do not adequately restrict access to their functionality. It is usually made possible through non-secured inter-app component communication channels [15]. It can result in a reduced forensic footprint since malware can perform the malign operation without explicitly requesting the associated permission or feature. However, the ability to carry out this capability leak attack is not very dependable as it usually relies on insecure coding on the part of the third-party app developer and requires the vulnerable app to be installed on the device at the point of malware execution.

One particularly sought-after attack vector comprises vulnerabilities inside system code, whose exploitation result in device rooting [16]. However, while extremely powerful, in terms of stealth, this approach can be very noisy.

2.2 The Accessibility Attack Vector

Android accessibility features are made available to any app requesting the BIND_ACCESSIBILITY_SERVICE permission. By simply sub-classing AccessibilityService, along with component registration, the app gains access to all GUI events of interest for any app. Its corresponding event handling code receives an AccessibilityEvent through which the GUI of a third-party app is abstracted as a tree of GUI elements along with all displayed information (possibly including credentials or other sensitive information) which are not protected by the importantForAccessibility mask. Apart from reading associated data, through the AccessibilityNodeInfo class, the accessibility service, in turn, can invoke further actions on the target app. While rendering every app on an Android device accessible to alternative means of interaction, accessibility services also introduced the nasty side-effect of potentially backdooring Android's security model.

This model is based on the principles of consent, isolation and containment [17] and it is surprising that it can be bypassed with a single abused permission [18] (Fig. 1). When compared to typical capability leaks, accessibility attacks are way more practical, from an attacker's point of view. This is, in large part, due to the feature being available on all devices and supported by all apps since UI elements have the isImportantForAccessibility flag set to auto by default [19].

Furthermore, recent malware [10] has shown how to fool Google's on-device scanner, Play Protect, through the use of accessibility as an attack vector. Since Play Protect was unable to detect the malicious code, this was therefore whitelisted as a trusted application on the Play Store.

The use of overlays [20] has been proposed to increase attack stealthiness by reducing the visibility of any accessibility attack. However, this work primarily focused on showing how overlays can be used to trick users into enabling accessibility and hide any nefarious actions after that. That being said, recent malware has shown that less sophisticated methods, such as using deceit in their user prompts can suffice.

2.3 Living Off the Land (LotL)

Campbell et al. [13] first introduced and coined the concept of LotL, even though several previous attacks already made use of this approach. Through their work,

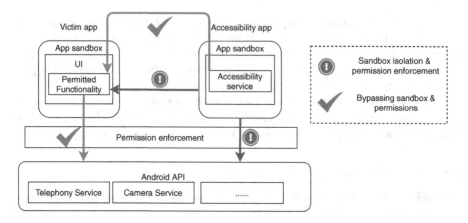

Fig. 1. The accessibility attack vector bypasses Android's permission and isolation-based security model.

they concluded that "using a few built-in tools and a healthy dose of Power-shell, an attacker can greatly reduce their forensic footprint". The underpinning principle of LotL remains that of using white-listed system components through which to attain the malign attack objectives, as opposed to introducing malware components on the target system. To demonstrate the approach, they showed how classical attacks such as keylogging, C2, and privilege escalation are carried out on Windows systems. They then went on to compare these attack implementations to what they referred to as a minimalist approach, whereby only using built-in system tools they managed to obtain the same malicious outcomes while reducing their forensic footprint. In some cases they managed to obtain a fileless posture whereby no malicious executables are placed on the file system.

Due to the nature of its target device install-base, Android lacks similar administrative tools to allow an analogous tactic to work. However, Android's accessibility services seem like the ideal substitute to implement a comparable strategy of providing access to all white-listed logic triggered via GUI actions. Even though such malware has to be delivered to the device in the form of an APK, subsequent attacks in this paper show that the APK may only be required during the initial stages of the attack, whit the following stages only requiring the white-listed apps.

2.4   Elaborate Cybercrime Schemes

Malware is not the only tool available to cybercriminals. There are more elaborate schemes involving some other sort of deceit or impersonation. One example made infamous in recent years due to its role in many attacks involving the looting of cryptocurrency funds is that of SIM-swapping [21]. A SIM swap comprises an attacker successfully convincing a mobile operator to switch the victim's phone number over to a different SIM card, one they own. By diverting the victim's incoming messages, scammers can easily complete the 2FA checks commonly needed for moving cryptocurrencies out of exchanges. While the implications of these attacks can be significant, they tend to leave a more extensive forensic footprint across different sources. For example, in the case of SIM-swapping forensic analysts can now also rely on evidence left at the mobile operator, from simple audit entries down to CCTV footage from the mobile operator outlet where the SIM-swapping request occurred.

2.5   Related Work

Obfuscation and anti-analysis [6] are popular approaches for achieving stealthiness while eluding detection at a malware sandbox level. However, detection and response tools can make use of deobfuscation [22] and other anti-anti-analysis tools and techniques to counter them. Yet some obfuscation techniques go to the extent of corrupting runtime structures to change the low-level semantics of the code [23], e.g. switch the behaviour of the innocuous `JSONObject` with that of `LocationManager`. While potentially bypassing app store and on-device scanning, access to the device location services, in this case, would ultimately get uncovered by any system API monitor. On the other hand, what would remain below the radar, even at this level of observation, is if malware delegated all of its location services misdemeanours to a benign app through accessibility services access.

While LotL is a well known stealth-enhancing threat on traditional platforms like MS Windows (with ongoing efforts towards novel LotL detection techniques [24]), not much work has focused on the possibility of LotL on Android. As a result, no LotL-specific analysis or forensic techniques have been studied or developed for Android. In this work, we are demonstrating that LotL can indeed be succesfully achieved on Android, through the abuse of accessibility services. Accessibility is a known threat on Android, and researchers are developing tools and techniques [19] aimed at mitigating some of these issues. However, the proposed measures are far from a complete solution to the problem and only tackle particular issues. Google developers have even tried to mitigate the threat by placing more stringent controls on the app store concerning accessibility apps. However, this decision had to be reverted [25] due to a backlash from the developer community.

Given the nature of accessibility, accessibility-enabled attacks can be found across platforms [26]. However, when compared to the second most popular mobile OS (iOS), Android attacks are much more prevalent due to the OS's accessibility design. As opposed to granting accessibility to any app requesting the relevant permission, iOS takes a significantly more conservative approach with its UIAutomation framework. This feature set is part of the private API set, made available only to pre-packaged apps, and therefore its use is forbidden to third-party apps uploaded to the Apple Store.

3   Accessibility Misuse

In this section, we will explain the general steps involved in a standalone accessibility attack, as well as the steps required in a comprehensive accessibility attack scenario which consists of several standalone accessibility attacks. We will then explain the different use cases of SMS abuse, C2-equipped malware, and crypto exchange theft, comparing implementations of a classical, non-accessibility implementation to different accessibility-enabled implementations.

3.1   Threat Model

The relevant attacks for our work deal with hiding post-infection activity from detection and response tools. We assume that a malicious accessibility app managed to make its way to a user's device undetected, and was subsequently granted the necessary permissions by the end-user. Surveys about malware in the wild have shown, time and again, that this scenario occurs way more frequently than what one would hope [27]. In the following sub-sections we first describe the attack steps common to any accessibility attacks aiming at transforming existing attacks into stealthier ones, we then present the specific use-cases of SMS abuse, C2-equipped malware, and a crypto exchange theft.

3.2   Setting up Malicious Accessibility Services

Having a malicious accessibility service delegate functionality to a target victim app, or else attacking it directly in a malware-only setting, proceeds as follows. First, the app hosting the malicious accessibility service launches the victim app. This can be done using an `Intent` object, which is a predominantly asynchronous messaging component Android developers can use to request an action from another app component. Next, the accessibility service idles, waiting for the victim app to appear in the foreground. This event can be picked up by the appropriate filter being set inside the overridden `onAccessibilityEvent()` handler, at which point it can gain access to the relevant UI elements, e.g. buttons or edit texts. Subsequently, the accessibility service proceeds to traverse the tree of `AccessibilityNodeInfo` elements, calling `performAction()` among multiple other ways, to interact with the victim application.

For example, to exploit this flow for SMS abuse, the accessibility malware can first launch the default SMS app, passing the destination number and message text inside the `Intent` parameters. Next, the accessibility service starts monitoring the foreground activity, waiting for the SMS app to be in the foreground. Once it is, the accessibility service looks for the "send" button. It automatically completes the task by "clicking" on it through a `performAction()` call, without having to bring it to the user's attention.

A comprehensive accessibility attack scenario ultimately comprises an entire sequence of such mimicked user actions, and with three main stages (see Fig. 2), where each one encompasses one or more accessibility attacks. The first one is the

Configuration stage where the malware, once having tricked the user into granting the accessibility permission, proceeds to download the victim app, followed by any required user registration and after disabling notifications for additional stealth. All these steps can be carried out through accessibility services, and of course, are only required if the app is not already available on the device. The next *Malicious Operation* stage is victim-app-specific. It performs the interaction mentioned above steps, multiple times, to leverage whatever app functionality appeals to the attacker. The final *Evidence Removal* stage can optionally delete all remnants belonging to the attack steps, for example deleting any compromising sent SMS text message from its corresponding chat. However, it may be the case that the nature of the attack requires that the sent text message should be left on the device in order to confuse incident response.

It is noteworthy that the final *Evidence Removal* stage may even proceed to remove the malware app itself even before the attack is over. This could be the case where the victim app is one that provides some form of remote control, or else some kind of scheduled task, over the infected device. We refer to this scenario as *Full LotL*, meaning that the attacker manages to attain a malware-less posture on the device during an ongoing attack. In the upcoming use cases, we demonstrate two examples that abuse SMSonPC apps such as the popular Pushbullet app and remote administration apps such as the Teamviewer app for a similar purpose.

Even though the underlying accessibility service initiating the attack is running in the background, the accessibility attacks often force the victim app to run in the foreground. This can result in the victim seeing what is going on. However, through the use of overlay and speed tactics, we were able to reduce the impact of foreground activity further. The use of overlays to hide malicious activity has been proven to be very effective in hiding accessibility attacks [20].

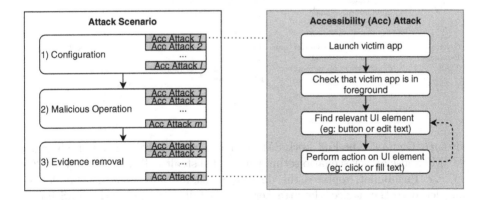

Fig. 2. Accessibility attack scenario stages.

3.3   SMS Abuse Attack

Non-accessibility Version. On Android, two approaches allow apps to send SMSs. The first involves requesting the SEND_SMS permission and calling sendTextMessage() through SmsManager. The second involves using the default SMS app and passing an intent with the appropriate message parameters. The former is typically the preferred method since the latter requires user confirmation upon every SMS sending. It is worth noting that, in more recent Android versions, an SMS sending app is not allowed to delete an SMS unless the user explicitly configures the app as the default SMS application.

LotL Version. Through accessibility, a LotL version of the same attack becomes possible. The LotL SMS scenario in Table 1 describes the setup for each of the accessibility attack scenario stages, with the attacker sending text messages over SMS through the default messaging app. As opposed to the non-accessibility approach, this version does not require SEND_SMS permission or any of the associated API methods.

Table 1. Accessibility attack scenarios († = Accessibility attack)

Scenario	Configuration	Malicious operation	Evidence removal
LotL SMS	Targets default SMS app No config required	Send SMS†	Delete SMS†
Full LotL SMS	Install SMSonPC (Pushbullet)† Enable Permissions† Disable Notifications† Login SMSonPC†	Send SMS through SMSonPC	Remove trojan† OR Delete SMS†
LotL C2	Targets default web-browser No config required	Navigate to white-listed website†	Delete history†
Full LotL C2	Install Remote Admin app (Teamviewer)† Enable permissions† Disable notifications† Login to Teamviewer†	Exfiltrate files from storage through Teamviewer remote control functionality	Remove trojan†
Crypto Exchange Theft	Assumes that the victim apps are already installed No configuration is required	Obtain 2FA token from 2FA app† Perform withdrawal (passing 2FA as params)†	Remove trojan†

Full LotL Version. The Full LotL SMS scenario in Table 1 describes an alternative SMS abuse attack scenario setup, with added stealth. This time a SMSonPC app, e.g. Pushbullet, replaces the default messaging app. Once Pushbullet is smuggled onto the device, the attacker obtains full control over the SMS functionality on the victim device, and the malware is no longer required and thus deleted. We use the term Full LotL to refer to the fact that at this point, the attacker makes exclusive use of a benign app to successfully pull off the attack, without the need for malware persistence.

3.4   C2-Equipped Malware

Non-accessibility C2. Widely deployed banking trojans typically come equipped with a C2 channel, providing attackers remote control over infected devices, with Android malware being no exception [10,11]. While C2 channels can be used for all sorts of communication, exfiltration of stolen credentials as part of a phishing attack is a frequent feature in banking trojans. On the other hand, in Android, the shared storage location is used to store selfies, screenshots, and miscellaneous multimedia files. The READ_EXTERNAL_STORAGE permission is required for such operations. Transferring all stolen data back to the C2 server requires a custom network protocol or, preferably leveraging widely-used cloud messaging infrastructures, e.g. Firebase Cloud Messaging. HTTP tends to be the application protocol of choice, due to its compatibility with firewall settings. Whatever the approach, malware needs to request the INTERNET permission.

LotL C2. The LotL C2 scenario in Table 1 describes one possible setup for the different accessibility attack scenario stages, in order to employ a stealthy LotL C2 channel. In this case, the attacker uses the default web browser to send and receive data from the victim's device. An advantage of this approach is that it does not require any extra permissions requests since they are already granted to the browser. Furthermore, malware can circumvent even the strictest URL black-list by connecting to a white-listed website rather than connecting directly to the C2 server.

Full LotL C2 . Setting up a stealthy C2 can even be pushed further, for example, not requiring any malware to be present on the device beyond the configuration stage. As shown in the Full LotL C2 scenario shown in Table 1, the accessibility malware can simply install a white-listed remote administration app to control the device and exfiltrate user data.

3.5   Crypto Exchange Theft

SIM Swapping. A SIM swap is when someone convinces a mobile operator to switch the victim's phone number over to a SIM card they own. By diverting the victim's incoming messages, scammers can easily complete the text-based 2FA checks that typically protect crypto exchange accounts. In combination with stolen passwords from a phishing attack, this leaves the victim's crypto wallet up for grabs.

Malware-Only Attack. 2FA-bypassing malware is the holy grail of banking trojans. An Android accessibility abuse makes this possible. The setup of this scenario is shown in the Crypto Exchange Theft scenario in Table 1. In this case, it is noteworthy that SMS 2FA tokens are gradually being replaced by more secure alternatives [28], with 2FA apps being the most popular choice. However, even these can be bypassed with accessibility attacks, in the same spirit. Perhaps only hardware tokens or biometric-based ones present an exception, although creative social engineering tricks can probably overcome these extra (and as yet uncommon) security measures.

In this scenario, the accessibility trojan obtains the 2FA token from the 2FA app or SMS and then passes the stolen token as a parameter in the withdrawal process. Fig. 3 shows how after using an intent to launch the 2FA app (Google Authenticator), the trojan reads the text value of the token by finding the text value of the view `com.google.android.apps.authenticator2:id/pin_value` using the accessibility command `findAccessibilityNodeInfosByViewId`. After obtaining the 2FA token, the malware then opens the victim's exchange app and clicks its way through the withdrawal process. Once the 2FA entry is prompted, the trojan then passes the stolen value in the appropriate edit text.

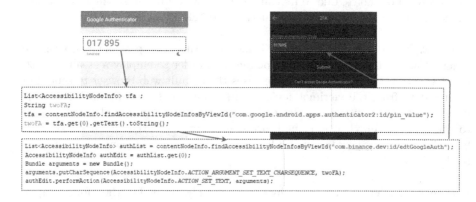

Fig. 3. 2FA token theft and use.

4   Forensic Footprint Comparisons

Here we demonstrate the reduced forensic footprint in all of our attack examples, by comparing the artefacts left behind in each case. The forensic footprint is compared across several analysis probes. Unless noted otherwise, all sources of evidence are supplied by MobSF probes. All attacks were executed on actual Android devices (Nexus 5x, Samsung Galaxy S8, and Samsung A30s) as well as on Android emulators ranging from Android API levels 23 to 29. The artefacts taken into consideration are as follows: APK-derived requested Permissions (P), and API and Library classes/methods (ALc); Sandbox execution-derived API and Library method calls invoked (ALe), Network traffic (N), non-Volatile Memory (nVM) data, Logcat (L) and Dumpsys (D) entries.

We ranked the outcome of the forensic footprint for each of the artefacts between 0–2. A 0 label indicates that the malware does not leave any forensic footprint behind. In contrast, a value of 2 indicates that there is enough forensic footprint to attribute the malicious behaviour to the malware through clear evidence. A value of 1 indicates that a forensic footprint exists, however it does not suffice to attribute the malicious behaviour to the malware. In the cases of probes P and ALc, attribution is determined through the binary on which the analysis is occurring. Whereas the remaining probes depend on process IDs for attribution. Additionally, N also makes use of process ID and src/dest port correlation, and nVM makes use of the app's local storage.

All attacks from Sect. 3 were implemented in the Metasploit pentest framework, as part of the Android Meterpreter payload. The post-exploitation commands used were `send_sms` for SMS sending and commands from the `stdapi` command set such as `download` for C2 data exfiltration. The accessibility attacks required an alternative implementation for each of them, specifically targeting: Pushbullet (package: com.pushbullet.android, ver:18.2.35) and Google Messages (package: com.google.android.apps.messaging, ver:5.7.097) in the case of SMS sending, and Teamviewer Host (package: com.teamviewer.host.market, ver: 15.6.51) and Google Chrome (package: com.android.chrome, ver:81.0.4044.117) in the case of C2. Finally, the Crypto exchange theft was tested on Binance (package: com.binance.dev, ver:1.21.1).

4.1 Results

SMS Abuse. Figure 4 shows the SMS abuse forensic footprint comparison results. It reveals LotL's reduced forensic footprint across the various probes. One instance where the LotL approach leaves more forensic evidence than the non-accessibility approach is the network activity during the Pushbullet attack. This observation is due to Pushbullet having first to receive a network command before it can send text messages. That said, the network activity is not attributed to the malicious accessibility app, but rather to Pushbullet. In fact, in this Full LotL attack version, the accessibility malware is not even on the device anymore at the point when the text messages are sent.

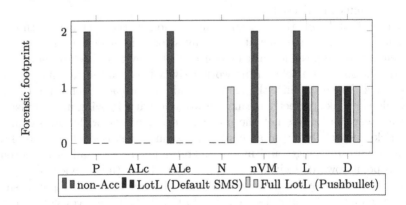

Fig. 4. Forensic footprints - SMS abuse attacks.

C2-Equipped Malware. Figure 5 shows the C2 forensic footprint comparison, clearly displaying LotL's reduced forensic footprint across the various probes.

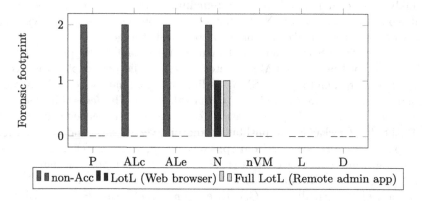

Fig. 5. Forensic footprints - C2-equipped malware attacks.

Crypto Exchange Theft. Had a SIM-swapping approach been followed for pulling off this attack, the expected result is one where the attacker ample leaves forensic evidence at the mobile provider, possibly including CCTV footage of the person buying the SIM. Moreover, at the exchange site, new logs originating from the attacker's IP rather than the victim's could also be observed. That is one of the reasons why Binance triggers an alarm every time an authentication request comes from new/unknown IP addresses. Once IP data is obtained, forensic analysts can even dig deeper and request service provider logs to identify the source of the crime. Cybercriminals can make use of tools like anonymous proxies or VPNs in order to cover their tracks, however, an alarm will still be triggered for every new/unknown IP used.

On the other hand, the malware-only version of the exchange withdrawal attack has the advantage that it only leaves forensic evidence on the device, and even in this case, the forensic evidence on the device is already significantly reduced. The only left artefact is network activity between the victim device and the exchange. However, since the victim would have already been using the app, this would seem like perfectly normal network activity. Proving in a forensically sound manner that it was not the user who executed the withdrawal could be quite tricky, especially if the accessibility trojan is removed afterwards. From the ISP, crypto exchange, and mobile operator perspective, all of the forensic artefacts point towards legitimate activity from the victim's device. This could be very problematic when dealing with cases of financial fraud. Figure 6 shows the forensic footprint comparison results. In this case, we also consider external sources, namely: ISP, crypto exchange (CE), and mobile operator (MO).

We have responsibly disclosed the possibility of these attacks to two of the most popular crypto exchanges, and both acknowledged the issue. To their credit,

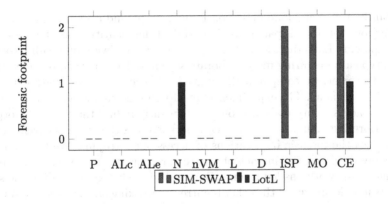

Fig. 6. Forensic footprints - Crypto exchange theft.

after our communication and only in a matter of days Binance took appropriate measures by disabling the accessibility feature for critical UI elements involved in the withdrawal process. We tested the attack against the updated version of their application and confirmed that it was able to block our initial accessibility withdrawal attack. The other exchange awarded us a bug bounty on the Hackerone platform [29] and seems to be in the process of mitigating the issue. It is important to note that this is not necessarily a bug or vulnerability from the part of the exchanges, but rather an OS feature that can be easily misused for stealing funds if no new countermeasures are implemented.

5   Discussion and Conclusion

Given the potential for stealthiness in accessibility attacks, their forensic analysis requires not only leveraging the state-of-the-art in mobile forensics but also extending it further concerning ephemeral evidence inside volatile memory. Stealthy malware is unlikely to leave any traces on disk. However, it cannot avoid leaving marks on volatile memory at one point or another. The likely brief presence in memory of relevant artefacts, which could be indicators of compromise, call for a just-in-time collection approach [30]. The challenges with this strategy are, nevertheless, many. The memory collection has to be done in a timely manner, and overheads have to be kept minimal while still being able to locate and parse the required evidence. Additionally, the method employed must ensure that it does not cause the app to crash nor allow the malware to detect that the analysis is taking place. In terms of prevention, hardened authentication mechanisms such as physical 2FA tokens and interactive CAPTCHAs can help reduce the risk of malicious apps performing sensitive operations on the user's behalf.

Accessibility apps have become a "double-edged sword", as they bring significant security threats to users. Malicious accessibility apps are able to perform sensitive operations by hijacking trusted white-listed apps easily, and more importantly, they can elude detection by leaving behind a significantly reduced forensic footprint. In this paper, we first studied the security risks of accessibility apps employing LotL tactics, and those that offer a malware-only substitute for attacks typically requiring more elaborate schemes. To demonstrate the reduced forensic footprint, we compared the analysis of accessibility malware with non-accessibility variants. The experimental results showed that across several analysis probes, accessibility malware could significantly reduce the forensic footprint when performing malign operations. Our work exposes the severe security threats and outlines the forensic implications of accessibility trojans. We have notably responsibly disclosed the impact of our research on two major cryptocurrency exchanges. Our work has led to one (Binance) immediately upgrading the security of its mobile app while the other is currently working on it. Given the severity of the threats posed, as well as the powerful stealth capabilities of accessibility attacks, Google may need to reconsider the openness of its accessibility services in the short term, before cybercriminals start exploiting them widely.

Acknowledgement. This work is supported by the LOCARD Project under Grant H2020-SU-SEC-2018-832735.

References

1. Zdnet: Bigger than Windows, bigger than iOS (2019). https://www.zdnet.com/article/bigger-than-windows-bigger-than-ios-google-now-has-2-5-billion-active-android-devices-after-10-years/
2. Gdata: Cyber attacks on Android devices on the rise (2018). https://www.gdatasoftware.com/blog/2018/11/31255-cyber-attacks-on-android-devices-on-the-rise
3. Hutchinson, S., Zhou, B., Karabiyik, U.: Are we really protected? An investigation into the play protect service. In: 2019 IEEE BigData, pp. 4997–5004. IEEE (2019)
4. Alepis, E., Patsakis, C.: Hey doc, is this normal?: Exploring Android permissions in the post Marshmallow era. In: Ali, S.S., Danger, J.-L., Eisenbarth, T. (eds.) SPACE 2017. LNCS, vol. 10662, pp. 53–73. Springer, Cham (2017). https://doi.org/10.1007/978-3-319-71501-8_4
5. ENISA: Mobile Threats and Incident Handling (2015)
6. Petsas, T., et al.: Rage against the virtual machine: hindering dynamic analysis of Android malware. In: EuroSec 2014, pp. 1–6 (2014)
7. Alepis, E., Patsakis, C.: Trapped by the UI: the Android case. In: Dacier, M., Bailey, M., Polychronakis, M., Antonakakis, M. (eds.) RAID 2017. LNCS, vol. 10453, pp. 334–354. Springer, Cham (2017). https://doi.org/10.1007/978-3-319-66332-6_15
8. Ahmad, M., Khan, M.N.A.: A review of forensic analysis techniques for Android phones. JISR **15**(1), 23–30 (2017)
9. Diao, W., et al.: Kindness is a risky business: on the usage of the accessibility APIs in Android. In: 22nd RAID 2019, pp. 261–275 (2019)
10. Stefanko, L.: Insidious Android malware gives up all malicious features but one to gain stealth (2020). https://www.welivesecurity.com/2020/05/22/insidious-android-malware-gives-up-all-malicious-features-but-one-gain-stealth/

11. Threat Fabric: 2020 - Year of the RAT (2020). https://www.threatfabric.com/blogs/2020_year_of_the_rat.html
12. Techcrunch: Eventbot (2020). https://techcrunch.com/2020/04/29/eventbot-android-malware-banking
13. Campbell, C., Graeber, M.: Living Off the Land: A Minimalist's Guide to Windows Post-Exploitation (2013). http://www.securitybsides.com/w/page/67875719/BSidesAugusta
14. Zhou, Y., Jiang, X.: Dissecting android malware: characterization and evolution. In: 2012 IEEE SSP, pp. 95–109. IEEE (2012)
15. Yang, K., et al.: IntentFuzzer: detecting capability leaks of android applications. In: 9th ACM CCS, pp. 531–536 (2014)
16. Zhang, H., She, D., Qian, Z.: Android root and its providers: a double-edged sword. In: 22nd ACM SIGSAC, pp. 1093–1104 (2015)
17. Mayrhofer, R., et al.: The Android platform security model. CoRR abs/1904.05572 (2019). arXiv: 1904.05572
18. Kalysch, A., Bove, D., Müller, T.: How Android's UI security is undermined by accessibility. In: Proceedings of the 2nd Reversing and Offensive-oriented Trends Symposium, pp. 1–10 (2018)
19. Naseri, M., et al.: AccessiLeaks: investigating privacy leaks exposed by the Android accessibility service. Proc. PETs **2019**(2), 291–305 (2019)
20. Fratantonio, Y., et al.: Cloak and dagger: from two permissions to complete control of the UI feedback loop. In: 2017 IEEE (SP), pp. 1041–1057. IEEE (2017)
21. Serapiglia, A.: Cybersecurity and cryptocurrencies: introducing ecosystem vulnerabilities through current events. In: EDSIG ISSN, vol. 2473, p. 3857 (2019)
22. Kan, Z., et al.: Automated deobfuscation of Android native binary code. arXiv preprint arXiv:1907.06828 (2019)
23. Yang, X., et al.: How to make information-flow analysis based defense ineffective: an ART behavior-mask attack. In: Nguyen, P., Zhou, J. (eds.) ISC 2017. LNCS, vol. 10599, pp. 269–287. Springer, Cham (2017). https://doi.org/10.1007/978-3-319-69659-1_15
24. Velasco, L., Duijn, R.: Fileless-threats-analysis-and-detection. In: Dearbytes (2018)
25. Zdnet: Google pauses removal of apps that want to use accessibility services (2017). https://www.zdnet.com/article/google-pauses-crackdown-of-accessibility-api-apps/
26. Jang, Y., et al.: A11y attacks: exploiting accessibility in operating systems. In: Proceedings of the 2014 ACM SIGSAC, pp. 103–115 (2014)
27. Faruki, P., et al.: Android security: a survey of issues, malware penetration, and defenses. IEEE Commun. Surv. Tutor. **17**(2), 998–1022 (2014)
28. Drozhzhin, A.: SMS-based two-factor authentication is not safe-consider these alternative 2FA methods instead (2020). https://www.kaspersky.com/blog/2fa-practical-guide/24219/
29. Hackerone: Hackerone. https://www.hackerone.com/
30. Vella, M., Rudramurthy, V.: Volatile memory-centric investigation of SMS-hijacked phones: a Pushbullet case study. In: 2018 FedC- SIS, pp. 607–616. IEEE (2018)

A Novel Machine Learning Methodology for Detecting Phishing Attacks in Real Time

Vishal Arora[✉][ID] and Manoj Misra

Indian Institute of Technology Roorkee, Roorkee 247667, India
arora.v.vishal032@gmail.com, manojfec@gmail.com

Abstract. Phishing is a cybercriminal activity where the criminal masquerades as a trusted entity and attacks the righteous users to gain personal information illegally. Many phishing detection techniques have been proposed in the past which use blacklist/whitelist, heuristic, search engine, visual similarity and machine learning. The statistics say that the average lifespan of any phishing website is 8–10 h which makes it strenuous for most of the above-mentioned techniques to identify and detect it accurately. Blacklist/whitelist and Search Engine based techniques work in real time but may fail to handle zero day phishing attacks. To tackle this problem, it is essential to have an approach that studies the dynamic behavior of the websites and predicts the new phishing website accurately. Machine Learning has been used in the past to handle dynamic behavior of phishing websites. In this paper, we propose a method in which a browser extension makes an API call to the pre-trained machine learning model to fetch the results, thus making machine learning work in real-time. Six machine learning classifiers have been rigorously trained and tested on a dataset of 5430 legitimate URLs and 5147 phished URLs. We have used a novel feature in which HTTPS URLs can be accurately identified as phished or legitimate based on Certificate validation. This method also detects the phishing websites hidden behind the short URLs along with the normal URLs, thus making it more robust. This methodology has a quick response time of 1.74 s along with an accuracy of 99.93% which is better than the previous works.

Keywords: Phishing · Machine learning · Certificate validation · Decision Tree · Random Forest · Adaboost · Gradient Boost · KNN · Linear Discriminant Analysis

1 Introduction

With the growing use of the Internet in today's world, personal information is the key to providing the data of one's interest. This vast availability of personal information on the Internet acts as an opportunity to a cybercriminal, who then uses this crucial information to convert an attack into a crime. Phishing

© Springer Nature Switzerland AG 2020
K. Markantonakis and M. Petrocchi (Eds.): STM 2020, LNCS 12386, pp. 39–54, 2020.
https://doi.org/10.1007/978-3-030-59817-4_3

is a new age crime that employs social engineering to steal the unwary victim's personal data which includes financial company secrets, identity information, account credentials. Righteous users are fooled in which the social engineering schemes make them believe that they are being dealt with the original and trusted legitimate party.

As per the report published by Anti Phishing Working Group (APWG) [4], "Almost three-quarters of all phishing sites now use SSL protection, highest recorded since early 2015, and an indicator that users can't rely on SSL alone to understand whether a site is safe or not". APWG detected that the total number of phishing sites in the fourth quarter for the year 2019 was 162,115. The numbers indicate that it is the need of the hour to have a technique that can detect HTTPS phishing websites accurately.

To tackle these phishing attacks various techniques have been proposed. These techniques can be grouped into the following categorizations:

Blacklist and Whitelist Based Techniques: Blacklist contains URLs of the phishing websites and Whitelist contains URLs of the legitimate websites. The URL which is being visited is compared to the list of URLs. The webpage gets downloaded only when its URL is found/not found in the whitelist/blacklist. These techniques result in high false positives and false negatives and require that these lists are updated frequently to tackle novel phishing attacks.

Heuristic Based Techniques: These techniques detect phishing attacks by extracting various features such as logo extraction, URL length, etc from the phishing websites. These techniques are low in terms of accuracy as all phishing websites do not have common features. Additionally, it is easier to bypass these techniques once the features used are known to the attacker.

Search Engine Based Techniques: The popularity of a website is determined by the use of search engine based techniques. The popularity can be extracted by the use of URLs, the text on the given page, and also by the images available on the web page. Based on the popularity, a web page is identified as phished or legitimate. If the right set of keywords are not fed to the search engine, then this technique may result in high false positives.

Visual Similarity Based Techniques: These techniques compare phishing website's image with the legitimate website's image stored in its database for identification. These techniques have high time complexity as well as high storage needs.

Machine Learning Based Techniques: A collection of features is extracted from the website to form a dataset. Machine Learning algorithms are then trained with the newly formed dataset to create a model. The model makes predictions when fed with unseen data. These techniques can identify Zero-day phishing attacks accurately.

The goal of this research is to propose a methodology to detect phishing attacks using Machine Learning in real-time. Machine learning in real-time has been implemented in the past but the proposed method is better when compared in terms of accuracy. In addition the paper makes the following other research contributions.

The proposed method uses a novel feature in which certificate validation level is considered to detect HTTPS phishing websites with a false positive rate of 0.0024%. Our methodology also detects phishing websites hidden behind the short URLs.

The proposed method makes use of 11 features which include URL based features and third party based features. Six Machine Learning classifiers are trained and tested on these features to evaluate the performance of the model.

This paper has been organized into seven sections. The first section gives a brief introduction about the phishing attacks and the importance of phishing detection solutions. The second section explores the basic terminologies that have been used. The third section elaborates on the related work that has been done in this field so far. The fourth section explains the proposed approach for detecting phishing sites using machine learning algorithms. This section also explains the feature vector and how the short URL is handled. The fifth section deals with the experiments performed and the inference from the results of the experiments. The sixth section concludes the paper and discusses the future work. The seventh section emphasizes on the limitations of the proposed work.

2   Basic Terminologies

2.1   Machine Learning Algorithms

Decision Tree. A Decision tree [13] is a classification algorithm whose output is generated as a binary tree structure. Each internal node in this decision tree represents a test on the feature, each branch represents a specific outcome and the class label is represented by every leaf node. The entire path set from root to leaf is referred to as a classification rule set.

K Nearest Neighbors (KNN). KNN [14] is a classification algorithm in which the elements with similar characteristics are clustered. The class of a testing sample is predicted based upon the k neighbors which are closest to it. Euclidean distance is used to calculate the proximity of a test data point from training data.

Linear Discriminant Analysis. A powerful tool that is used for classification and dimensionality reduction is known as Linear Discriminant Analysis [12]. A linear transformation of the samples is found out from the given dataset of search results. The performance of the LDA is good if the features are linearly independent.

Random Forest. Random Forest [7] is an ensemble classification algorithm. Decision trees are used to predict in this algorithm. Class prediction is achieved by a number of decision trees that are constructed during the training phase. The classes obtained as a result of all the individual trees are clustered and the class having the highest vote is considered as an appropriate output.

Adaboost. In Adaboost [9], a number of weak algorithms(decision trees) with a set of weights are combined and learned as a strong algorithm by adaptive boost.

Each training set is assigned some weight when a classifier is trained at any level. Higher weight is assigned to the wrongly classified item. Hence, it appears with a higher probability in the next training set. When all the classifiers are trained, it assigns weight to each classifier based on its accuracy. Higher weight is assigned to the more accurate classifier.

Gradient Boost. Gradient Boost [15] is a regression and classification machine learning technique in which a prediction model is produced where weak prediction models (decision trees) are ensembled. Its working involves three stages. First, optimization of differentiable loss functions like logarithmic loss, squared error, etc. Second, choosing to constrain the weak learners based on nodes splits, leaf nodes, or the number of levels. Third, constructing an additive model where the addition of trees is done one at a time. To minimize the loss while adding trees, a gradient descent procedure is used in which parameters are first assigned to the tree, and then they are modified at every step to reduce residual loss. Once the loss reaches an acceptable value or it no longer improves, the training process stops.

2.2   Certificate Validation

To acquire a certificate [8], a user can opt for one of the three types of certificates based on the level of background verification. There are three types of certificate validations namely:

- Domain Validation
- Organization Validation
- Extended Validation

Domain Validation. If the purchaser can demonstrate to manage a domain name, which fulfills important background criteria, then the domain validation certificate will be issued by the certificate provider. It is the lowest level of assurance issued by the certificate provider.

Organization Validation. Organization Validation is issued to the purchaser by the certificate provider if the following two criteria are met. First, the purchaser demonstrates to manage a domain name. Second, the organization exists as a legal identity. It is an enhanced level of assurance issued by the certificate provider.

Extended Validation. In Extended Validation, the certificate provider conducts the thorough background verification of the organizational entity and the purchaser should also demonstrate to manage a domain name. It also includes manual verification in which the checks are carried out by a human.

With the help of a policy identifier, these levels of validations can be uniquely identified.

3   Related Work

Pan and Ding's [19] anti-phishing model uses DOM objects to extract the website's identity. These elements are keyword description, Server form handler, Abnormal URL, Abnormal DNS record, etc. They used Support Vector Machine classifier by experimenting with multiple features. The addition of a search engine to this anti-phishing approach could have made it a better option for phishing detection.

CANTINA [24] technique uses the term frequency and inverse document frequency algorithm. This algorithm operates on the website by using the textual content present on it. This algorithm extracts high TF-IDF score words. These score words are then given to the search engine to identify a phishing site. However, since this approach uses the textual content of the site, there is a deterioration in the performance of this approach and this approach can fail if the phished website textual content is replaced by the image of the snippet of the legitimate website.

Miyamoto and Kadobayashi [16] used nine Machine Learning algorithms to classify websites as legitimate or phished. Most of the features of the CANTINA model were incorporated to detect these sites. Of the nine Machine Learning algorithms, the best performance was given by the Adaboost algorithm with the highest f1 measure of 0.8581 and an accuracy of 93.42%. It has the same limitation as that of CANTINA i.e., if the textual content of the website is replaced by the image, this approach fails.

CANTINA+ [23] is an extension of the previously proposed CANTINA technique. In this technique, the Machine Learning algorithm called Bayesian Network is used to classify the phishing websites. This technique uses a two-level detection approach. The first level being the Hash-based near-duplicate page removal and login form detection. In the second level, they have fetched eight features that are URL based, HTML based, and web-based. Even though this technique is an extension to CANTINA, it still follows the same drawback i.e., if the textual content of the website is replaced by the image, this approach fails.

PhishAri [5] is a technique in which phishing URLs were detected in the tweets. The Random Forest classifier was used along with the URL based, WHOIS based, Tweet based, and Network-based feature sets. It was observed that the accuracy of the above phishing technique came down to 92.52% as compared to other techniques.

Gowtham and Krishnamurthi [11] used URL based features. Before applying heuristics they used two-level modules. In the first module, whitelist checks are done and the second module checks the presence of login form. They used 15 features and Support Vector classifier. These features are then fed to the classifier where the performance of the model is calculated. The accuracy observed by the use of this model is 99.61%. The above approach fails if the textual content of the website is replaced by the image.

Mohammad et al. [18] extracted website content and URL features. 17 features from the URL were extracted which were then used as an input to the neural network for classification. The model's performance can be improved by refreshing the training dataset frequently.

Moghimi and Varjani [17] extracted features from the website content. A browser extension was developed and the vector machine algorithm was used to detect phishing websites. This uses a rule-based technique. As this approach focuses more on the website content, the chances of failure increases when the website is modified or redesigned.

LPD [22] is a client-side search engine based approach. A query string is prepared out of the page title and the domain name of the URL. It is then fed to Google custom search and based on its presence in top 'k' results, it is classified as phished or legitimate. This approach fails when newly created domains are being inspected as they might not appear in the top list due to their short term existence.

LPD+ [21] is an extension to LPD. This technique follows an additional check on the already available technique LPD. The checks have been divided into three categories which are HTTPS logic check, domain name starting with a digit, and presence of URL in google's blacklist.

Table 1. Table of comparison of our work with the previous works

Work	Year	HTTPS	Short URLs	Classifier	Accuracy (%)	Real time
Pan and Ding [19]	2006	Not handled	No	SVM	90.00	No
CANTINA [24]	2007	Not handled	No	–	95.00	No
Miyamoto et al. [16]	2008	Not handled	No	Adaboost	93.42	No
CANTINA+ [23]	2011	Not handled	No	Bayesian Network	99.61	No
PhishAri [5]	2012	Not handled	No	Random Forest	92.52	Yes
Gowtham and Krishnamurthy [11]	2014	HTTPS & trusted authority means legitimate	No	SVM	99.61	No
Mohammad et al. [18]	2014	HTTPS & trusted authority means legitimate	No	Neural networks	92.48	No
Moghimi and Varjani [17]	2016	HTTPS means legitimate	No	SVM	98.65	Yes
LPD [22]	2016	Not handled	No	–	99.75	Yes
LPD+ [21]	2016	HTTPS means legitimate	No	–	99.29	Yes
Srinivasa and Roshan [20]	2018	HTTPS means legitimate	No	Random Forest	99.55	No
Proposed Work	**2020**	**Certificate Validation method**	**Yes**	**Gradient Boost**	**99.93**	**Yes**

Srinivasa and Roshan [20] extracted heuristic features that are divided into three categories namely URL based, HTML based, and the third party based. Random forest classifier was used to detect phishing website. The extraction of HTML based features degrades the performance of this method.

Table 1 summarizes the related work. It provides a comparison of previous works with our work based on the following five parameters. Detection of HTTPS phishing websites, detection of phishing websites hidden behind the short URLs, classifier used, accuracy and real-time working of the models.

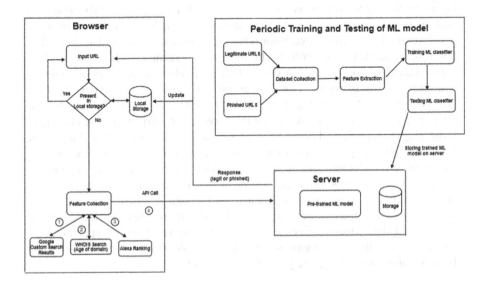

Fig. 1. System architecture

4 Proposed Work

4.1 System Architecture

Figure 1 represents the architecture of the proposed method. It comprises of three modules. The first module represents the periodic training and testing of the machine learning model. The second represents the server hosting the pre-trained machine learning model which is then exposed as an API (Application Programming Interface) and the third module represents the Chrome extension. For the system to work in real-time, Chrome Extension communicates with the server to get the predicted results and renders it onto the webpage.

- **Periodic Training and Testing of ML model.** At first, several phishing and legitimate URLs are collected. An automatic feature extractor is developed to extract the respective features of URLs. The extracted features form the dataset. The machine learning classifiers are then trained with the newly formed dataset. The model is trained periodically with the new dataset to ensure that the model is up to date. This trained model is then stored into the server database. Here, the Python language is used to train and test the model.

- **Server.** To make use of the classifier in real-time, a server is then created which exposes the stored pre-trained machine learning model as an API to give the predicted results.
- **Chrome Extension.** The necessity of Chrome extension arises as the user interacts with the web world through a client i.e., browser. To create an add on functionality on the existing browser, extensions can be used. Thus we developed a Chrome extension that acts as a firewall on the very first point of contact to the web world to detect phishing. When the URL is entered on the browser, the Chrome extension fetches the features and creates a feature vector using it. The feature vector is then passed to the REST (Representational State Transfer) API. Once the decision is made by the API, it returns the response as JSON (Javascript Object Notation) object indicating the predicted results. This set of activity completes during the time in which the page loads after the URL is entered onto the browser. The extension is developed using a javascript. With the help of Document Object Model, content scripts fetch the details of the webpage i.e., page title, URL, etc which are then used to create a feature vector.

The Chrome extension code can be easily ported to other browsers such as Microsoft Edge, Mozilla Firefox etc by replacing the browser specific APIs provided by Chrome developers with the equivalent available APIs of other browsers and by keeping the javascript APIs intact.

4.2   Feature Vector

Initially, several URL features were considered but based on their "feature importance" value [10], we finally considered the top 11 distinguishing features to create a feature vector. These features have been classified into URL based features and Third party based features.

URL Based Features. These features are extracted using Lexical analysis of the URL. In particular, features UBF1 and UBF2 are adopted from CANTINA [24]. Features UBF3, UBF4, UBF5 and UBF7 are adopted from [18]. Feature UBF6 is adopted from [17]. Specifically, feature UBF8 is the novel feature proposed by us in this research work.

- **UBF1: Number of dots in host name:** The hostname in the URL contains Geographical domain, TLD domain, primary domain, subdomain, etc. The domain of a legitimate website can be added as a subdomain of the phishing website by the attacker to deceive the users. Using a high number of dots hides the actual phished domain of the URL. This feature maintains the dot count in the hostname to identify the website's status.

- **UBF2: Presence of '@' symbol:** The presence of '@' symbol in the URL can be suspicious because whenever the web browser parses '@' symbol, everything before the symbol is ignored and address following '@' symbol is used. '@' symbol is added by the attackers after the legitimate domain and before the phished domain.
- **UBF3: Length of URL:** The attackers use a lengthy URL to hide the actual suspicious phishing domain. Many times they put the legitimate domain only in the pathname of the URL to gain the trust of the user whereas the hostname part contains the phishing domain. This feature calculates the length of URL to detect the true identity of a website.
- **UBF4: Presence of IP address:** The attackers use the IP address in place of a domain name in the URL to hide the suspicious phishing domain to trick the users. This binary feature examines the presence of the IP address in the URL.
- **UBF5: Presence of '−' symbol:** The attackers use the '−' symbol to impersonate the legitimate domain by simply placing it in between the words. This binary feature examines the presence of the '−' symbol in the URL.
- **UBF6: Length of domain:** This feature specifically calculates the length of the domain in the URL. As multiple subdomains can be used to a domain, criminals add a legitimate domain as the subdomain of the phishing domain to trick the users.
- **UBF7: protocol used:** HTTPS secured connections are used by most of the legitimate websites in case a piece of sensitive information is communicated. This feature examines the presence of protocol in the URL. If the protocol is HTTP, it is termed as phishing. If the protocol is HTTPS, then the certificate validation policy is checked.
- **UBF8: Certificate Validation:** As almost two-third of the phishing websites uses HTTPS connection, we used certificate validation level using the policy identifier present in the certificate. If the validation level is extended then it is classified as legitimate else it is classified as phished. This feature is significant as 77.5% of legitimate URLs use extended validation certificate policy.

Third Party Based Features. These features are extracted by making an API call to the third party server. In particular, TBF1 and TBF2 are adopted from [18]. TBF3 is adopted from CANTINA+ [23].

- **TBF1: Domain Age:** Newly registered domains are used to host most of the phishing domains. Phishing domains are either not present in the WHOIS [3] database or its age is less. A WHOIS API call is made to extract this feature.
- **TBF2: Alexa Ranking:** Alexa is a page ranking service that ranks the website based on its popularity, traffic, etc. As phishing websites have low popularity as compared to legitimate websites, we use this feature to detect the website's identity.
- **TBF3: Presence in Search Engine Results:** As suggested in LPD, keywords like page title, domain name are used to make a query string and are

given as input to the search engine. If the inspected domain is present in the list of top 10 domain names returned by the search engine, then it is termed as legitimate else phished.

4.3 Handling Short URLs

Shortening the URLs has become a popular trend as the breaking of the long URLs have become the need of an hour when these long URLs simply do not comply with the existing social networking trends. With the shortened URL, it is difficult to identify where the browser is pointed. Shortening the URL comes with its security risks which can be identified as follows:

- These urls can host a lot of malicious and malware programs.
- These short urls are a come home to a lot of phishing activity attempts that try to steal valuable information.

In a URL shortener service [6], there exists a database where the short URLs are stored and mapped to there related long URLs. When a browser communicates with the webserver, it issues a GET request to that short URL. In response, the URL shortener service looks up in its database. It returns a redirect response to the browser with the response code as 301 (moved permanently) or 302 (moved temporarily) along with the long URL in the location field of the response header. Upon receiving the response, the browser looks up the location field automatically and issues the GET request to the new long URL.

We have fetched the corresponding long URLs for the short URLs by interrupting the automatic redirection of the connection and fetching the long URL from the response header. Once the long URL is fetched, we then extracted the corresponding features of the feature vector and worked on it.

5 Experiments and Discussions

5.1 Dataset Used

To construct the model, we collected 5430 legitimate URLs from Alexa [1] database and 5147 phished URLs from phishtank [2] database. This dataset was further divided into a 70% training set and a 30% test set to evaluate the performance of our model.

5.2 Performance Metrics

For our experiments, we have considered positive as a situation when URL is detected as phished and negative as a situation when URL is detected as legitimate. By using the standard information retrieval metrics, we have evaluated the effectiveness of the method described. True Positive (TP) is the number of phished URLs that were correctly detected among the given set of URLs. True Negative (TN) is the number of benign URLs that were correctly detected as non-phished from the given set of URLs. False Positive (FP) is the number of benign URLs that were incorrectly identified as phished. False Negative (FN) is the number of phished URLs that were incorrectly identified as non-phished. The metrics that have been considered for performance evaluation are as follows:

- Precision: It is the ratio of true positives to the sum of true positives and false positives. The higher the precision the better the model.

$$Precision = \frac{TP}{TP + FP} \tag{1}$$

- Recall: It is the ratio of true positives to the sum of true positives and false negatives. The higher the recall the better the model.

$$Recall = \frac{TP}{TP + FN} \tag{2}$$

- f1 measure: It is the harmonic mean of precision and recall.

$$f1\ measure = \frac{2*Precision*Recall}{Precision + Recall} \tag{3}$$

- Specificity: It is the ratio of true negatives to the sum of true negatives and false positives.

$$Specificity = \frac{TN}{TN + FP} \tag{4}$$

- Accuracy: It is the ratio of sum of true positives and true negatives to the total number of websites.

$$Accuracy = \frac{TP+TN}{TP+TN+FP+FN} \tag{5}$$

- Error rate: It is the ratio of sum of false positives and false negatives to the total number of websites.

$$Error\ rate = \frac{FP+FN}{TP+TN+FP+FN} \tag{6}$$

- Total time: It measures the total time taken by the proposed method to check the authenticity of the website. It is the sum of the maximum of time taken by whois API query, Alexa API query, google custom search API query, time taken to resolve short URLs, and the time taken by machine learning API.

$$T_{total} = \max(T_{whois}, T_{alexa}, T_{google}, T_{short}) + T_{ml} \tag{7}$$

5.3   Experimental Evaluation and Results

We tested our feature set on several machine learning classifiers out of which we have listed the top six classifiers based on their performance. Five experiments were conducted in total, out of which the first three compares the results of six machine learning classifiers over a common dataset to evaluate the performance of the model. The fourth experiment gives the timing analysis of the proposed method when it is tested on various URLs chosen randomly from the dataset. The fifth experiment analyzes the average running time of the proposed model with the average page load time when tested on a randomly chosen set of URLs.

Table 2. Evaluation of features without certificate validation feature

Classifier/metrics	Precision	Recall	f1 measure	Specificity	Accuracy	Error rate
Decision Tree	0.9981	0.9956	0.9968	0.9980	0.9968	0.0031
K Nearest Neighbours	0.9839	0.9821	0.9830	0.9818	0.9820	0.0179
Linear Discriminant Analysis	0.9914	0.9895	0.9904	0.9909	0.9902	0.0097
Random Forest	0.9975	0.9962	0.9968	0.9974	0.9968	0.0031
Adaboost	0.9962	0.9962	0.9962	0.9961	0.9962	0.0037
Gradient Boost	**0.9993**	**0.9975**	**0.9984**	**0.9993**	**0.9984**	**0.0015**

Experiment 1: Evaluation of Features Without Certificate Validation Feature. The certificate validation feature (UBF8) was excluded from this experiment. We analyzed the features with six machine learning classifiers to find out the best performing classifier. Gradient Boost classifier performed the best with an accuracy of 99.84%. The results are shown in Table 2.

Table 3. Evaluation of features without third party features

Classifier/metrics	Precision	Recall	f1 measure	Specificity	Accuracy	Error rate
Decision Tree	0.9754	0.9918	0.9836	0.9745	0.9832	0.0167
K Nearest Neighbours	0.9657	0.9816	0.9736	0.9629	0.9725	0.0274
Linear Discriminant Analysis	0.8428	0.9483	0.8925	0.8094	0.8815	0.1184
Random Forest	0.9760	0.9931	0.9845	0.9751	0.9842	0.0157
Adaboost	0.9449	0.9714	0.9580	0.9391	0.9558	0.0441
Gradient Boost	**0.9777**	**0.9920**	**0.9848**	**0.9758**	**0.9842**	**0.0157**

Experiment 2: Evaluation of Features Without Third Party Features. In this experiment, we excluded third party features (TBF1,TBF2 and TBF3) and analyzed the performance with different machine learning classifiers. When compared, it was observed that the accuracy was degraded to 98.42% which is why third party features are significant in our feature set. The results are shown in Table 3.

Table 4. Evaluation of features including all the 11 features

Classifier/metrics	Precision	Recall	f1 measure	Specificity	Accuracy	Error rate
Decision Tree	0.9981	0.9981	0.9975	0.9980	0.9981	0.0018
K Nearest Neighbours	0.9791	0.9863	0.9835	0.9781	0.9823	0.0176
Linear Discriminant Analysis	0.9926	0.9919	0.9923	0.9922	0.9921	0.0078
Random Forest	0.9969	0.9981	0.9972	0.9967	0.9974	0.0025
Adaboost	0.9962	0.9987	0.9965	0.9961	0.9974	0.0025
Gradient Boost	**0.9993**	**0.9993**	**0.9993**	**0.9993**	**0.9993**	**0.0006**

Experiment 3: Evaluation of Features Including All the 11 Features. In this experiment, all of the discussed features were included and analyzed with different machine learning classifiers. The results obtained were better than the results of experiments 1 and 2. Gradient Boost classifier performed the best with an accuracy of 99.93%. The results are shown in Table 4.

Experiment 4: Run Time Analysis. In this experiment, we recorded the best, the average, and the worst total time (T_{total}) when the working model is tested on various URLs. Table 5 represents the best, the average, and the worst timings recorded. On average, what percentage of each API call contributes to the total running time was also recorded in this experiment. The percentage when combined according to the formula 7 results to the total of 100%. The results can be seen in Table 6.

Table 5. Run time analysis of various urls from the dataset

Best time	Average time	Worst time
1.74 s	2.07 s	2.46 s

Table 6. Each API call's contribution to the total average running time

Whois api(%)	Alexa api(%)	Google api(%)	short url(%)	ml api(%)
83.00	42.00	55.00	18.00	17.00

Experiment 5: Average Page Load Time Vs Average Running Time of the Proposed Model. In this experiment, we compared the average running time of the proposed model with the average time a web page takes to load on the browser. When tested on a set of URLs, the average page load time recorded was 2.80 s. Although, page load time depends on various factors like average server delay, network latency, number of resources the standard web page loads, size of a web page, etc. It may vary if tested on a larger set of URLs. As the average running time of our model recorded was 2.07 s. It can be concluded that our model gives results within 74% of the total page load time.

Figure 2 represents the plot of accuracy obtained from different classifiers trained with all the 11 features.

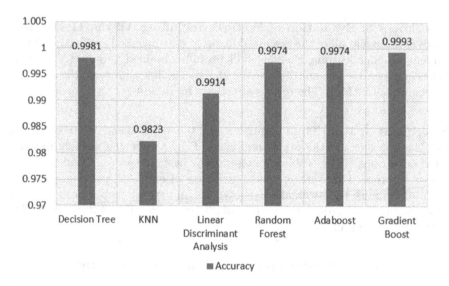

Fig. 2. A plot of accuracy obtained from six machine learning classifiers

6   Conclusions and Future Work

In this research, a novel real-time machine learning methodology to detect phishing websites has been proposed. A novel feature is proposed in which the certificate validation level is considered to detect HTTPS phishing websites. Also when the proposed method is compared to the previous works, it gives an accuracy of 99.93%. Along with this, short URLs are also considered for classification which is often neglected. Considering the need of an hour, this model also functions in real-time. A comparison of our work with the previous works based on accuracy, handling of short URLs, handling HTTPS URLs is shown in Table 1.

The proposed work also handles phishing websites in which the textual content is replaced by the snippet of the legitimate website. The list-based anti-phishing solutions fail to detect the zero hour phishing attacks whereas our approach detects these attacks. Any given Web page contains static as well as dynamic content, previous works that use source code of a webpage as a feature to identify its status fails in case of dynamic content. But this approach handles webpages with both static as well as dynamic content.

In the future, we aim to propose more URL based features so that the dependency on third party features is reduced. Also, javascript machine learning libraries which are still under development can be used instead of creating a dedicated server to improve the response time.

7   LIMITATIONS

The accuracy of the proposed method depends on the proper selection of features. Phishers may come up with different methods of phishing which may require reselection of features. For instance, earlier phishing websites were not using HTTPS but now most of them use HTTPS.

References

1. Alexa: The top 500 sites on the web (2020). https://www.alexa.com/topsites/. Accessed 12 March 2020
2. Phishtank: Developer information (2020). https://www.phishtank.com/developer_info.php/. Accessed 12 March 2020
3. WHOIS API: Unified and Consistent WHOIS Data (2020). https://whois.whoisxmlapi.com/. Accessed 20 March 2020
4. APWG: Phishing attack trends reports (2020). https://apwg.org/trendsreports/. Accessed 1 May 2020
5. Aggarwal, A., Rajadesingan, A., Kumaraguru, P.: PhishAri: automatic realtime phishing detection on Twitter. In: 2012 eCrime Researchers Summit, pp. 1–12. IEEE (2012)
6. Antoniades, D., et al.: we.b: the web of short urls. In: Proceedings of the 20th International Conference on World Wide Web, pp. 715–724 (2011)
7. Breiman, L.: Random forests. Mach. Learn. **45**(1), 5–32 (2001). https://doi.org/10.1023/a:1010933404324
8. Cooper, D., et al.: Internet X. 509 public key infrastructure certificate and certificate revocation list (CRL) profile. RFC 5280, pp. 1–151 (2008)
9. Freund, Y., Schapire, R.E.: A desicion-theoretic generalization of on-line learning and an application to boosting. In: Vitányi, P. (ed.) EuroCOLT 1995. LNCS, vol. 904, pp. 23–37. Springer, Heidelberg (1995). https://doi.org/10.1007/3-540-59119-2_166
10. Géron, A.: Hands-on Machine Learning with Scikit-Learn, Keras, and TensorFlow: Concepts, Tools, and Techniques to Build Intelligent Systems. O'Reilly Media (2019)
11. Gowtham, R., Krishnamurthi, I.: A comprehensive and efficacious architecture for detecting phishing webpages. Comput. Secur. **40**, 23–37 (2014)
12. Huh, J.H., Kim, H.: Phishing detection with popular search engines: simple and effective. In: Garcia-Alfaro, J., Lafourcade, P. (eds.) FPS 2011. LNCS, vol. 6888, pp. 194–207. Springer, Heidelberg (2012). https://doi.org/10.1007/978-3-642-27901-0_15
13. Kamiński, B., Jakubczyk, M., Szufel, P.: A framework for sensitivity analysis of decision trees. CEJOR **26**(1), 135–159 (2017). https://doi.org/10.1007/s10100-017-0479-6
14. Keller, J.M., Gray, M.R., Givens, J.A.: A fuzzy k-nearest neighbor algorithm. IEEE Trans. Syst. Man Cybern. **4**, 580–585 (1985)
15. Mason, L., Baxter, J., Bartlett, P.L., Frean, M.R.: Boosting algorithms as gradient descent. In: Advances in Neural Information Processing Systems, pp. 512–518 (2000)
16. Miyamoto, D., Hazeyama, H., Kadobayashi, Y.: An evaluation of machine learning-based methods for detection of phishing sites. In: Köppen, M., Kasabov, N., Coghill, G. (eds.) ICONIP 2008. LNCS, vol. 5506, pp. 539–546. Springer, Heidelberg (2009). https://doi.org/10.1007/978-3-642-02490-0_66
17. Moghimi, M., Varjani, A.Y.: New rule-based phishing detection method. Expert Syst. Appl. **53**, 231–242 (2016)

18. Mohammad, R.M., Thabtah, F., McCluskey, L.: Predicting phishing websites based on self-structuring neural network. Neural Comput. Appl. **25**(2), 443–458 (2013). https://doi.org/10.1007/s00521-013-1490-z
19. Pan, Y., Ding, X.: Anomaly based web phishing page detection. In: 2006 22nd Annual Computer Security Applications Conference (ACSAC 2006), pp. 381–392. IEEE (2006)
20. Rao, R.S., Pais, A.R.: Detection of phishing websites using an efficient feature-based machine learning framework. Neural Comput. Appl. **31**(8), 3851–3873 (2018). https://doi.org/10.1007/s00521-017-3305-0
21. Varshney, G., Misra, M., Atrey, P.K.: Improving the accuracy of search engine based anti-phishing solutions using lightweight features. In: 2016 11th International Conference for Internet Technology and Secured Transactions (ICITST), pp. 365–370. IEEE (2016)
22. Varshney, G., Misra, M., Atrey, P.K.: A phish detector using lightweight search features. Comput. Secur. **62**, 213–228 (2016)
23. Xiang, G., Hong, J., Rose, C.P., Cranor, L.: Cantina+ a feature-rich machine learning framework for detecting phishing web sites. ACM Trans. Inf. Syst. Secur. (TISSEC) **14**(2), 1–28 (2011)
24. Zhang, Y., Hong, J.I., Cranor, L.F.: Cantina: a content-based approach to detecting phishing web sites. In: Proceedings of the 16th International Conference on World Wide Web, pp. 639–648 (2007)

Confidentiality Schema

Revocable Access to Encrypted Message Boards

Fabian Schillinger$^{(\boxtimes)}$ and Christian Schindelhauer

Computer Networks and Telematics, Department of Computer Science,
University of Freiburg, Freiburg im Breisgau, Germany
{schillfa,schindel}@tf.uni-freiburg.de

Abstract. Online Social Networks are popular and play an important role in communication. In such networks, privacy is becoming increasingly important. Providers start to implement encryption procedures to ensure the privacy of users. Protocols for end-to-end encryption between two or multiple parties allow granting access to resources. However, access cannot easily be revoked, and negotiated keys cannot be withdrawn, using these protocols. They rely on re-encryption, using new keys and redistribution of content to ensure that undesired access is revoked. This paper aims to present protocols where distributed keys can be made unusable, such that re-encryption of ciphertexts is not needed. The protocols allow us to distribute and revoke symmetric and asymmetric keys. They are applicable for any content, that can be structured like a tree, like message boards, wikis, or online chats.

Keywords: End-to-end encryption · Message board · Online social network · Quorum · Proxy encryption

1 Introduction

The number of active Social Media users was more than 3.7 billion per month in October 2019 [6]. Facebook, as one of the largest Online Social Networks (OSNs) has over 1.6 billion daily active users [4]. Users of these networks can communicate through direct messages or by sharing content, like images, videos, websites, and others, with other users. For many of these communication channels, approaches to safeguard the privacy of users exist. These approaches often include encryption algorithms. Another way of communicating in OSNs is by creating groups or circles. Users can join a group if they think that the content of the group is interesting. These groups can be used comparable to message boards: different topics can be created, questions and answers can be posted. Websites, videos, images, and even collaborative wikis can be stored and shared in these groups. Sometimes they can be modified by other users in the group. Some groups are open to all users, others have restricted access. Especially in restricted groups, encryption can be used to protect the content and the privacy of the participants. However most approaches, using end-to-end encryption

© Springer Nature Switzerland AG 2020
K. Markantonakis and M. Petrocchi (Eds.): STM 2020, LNCS 12386, pp. 57–72, 2020.
https://doi.org/10.1007/978-3-030-59817-4_4

leave outside the possibilities on the one hand to allow end-to-end encryption between multiple parties, and on the other hand to revoke the access to these contents. The latter is an important property, especially in social groups with a fast-changing composition of participants. Every time someone leaves such a group the encryption has to change if keys cannot be revoked. If the keys are derived from each other, all content has to be re-encrypted using new keys.

Our Contribution

Our contribution consists of protocols to organize access to end-to-end encrypted message boards. The protocols can be used to grant and revoke access to groups, which are used in Online Social Networks. The protocols allow sharing encrypted data, as long as it can be organized in a tree-like structure. The protocols allow creating branches within the tree. Additionally, some branches can be private, or encrypted, whereas other branches might be publicly accessible.

The main advantage compared to other protocols is the possibility to easily revoke access. Decryption keys for the content are given to legitimate users. These keys can be made unusable. No explicit re-encryption of all content is needed to revoke the access. The revocable access can be used for specific users, or for multiple users. Another advantage is that access to encrypted content can be organized by a quorum of multiple users. Then, a user seeking access has to contact multiple users. This reduces the chance, that a vicious administrator denies all access requests.

Organization of the Paper

The paper is structured as follows: In Sect. 2 related work, regarding encrypted Online Social Networks, Quorum-based access structures, and Proxy-encryption are discussed. In Sect. 3 the backgrounds and model of the message board and the used cryptographic methods are described. In Sect. 4 our proposed protocols are described and analyzed in detail. The necessary discussions, regarding the security of our protocols, are given in Sect. 5. Finally, Sect. 6 concludes the work and gives an outlook on possible extensions.

2   Related Work

Different schemes are used for end-to-end encryption of messages between users. Often, asymmetric encryption protocols are used to exchange keys between users. These keys are used for symmetric encryption. Some of these protocols and approaches are discussed in the following. *Off-the-record* (OTR) [12] is a protocol which ensures end-to-end encrypted messaging. OTR can be used in instant messaging (IM) services, where messages are delivered in-order. Two senders X and Y each generate private keys $x_1, x_2, \ldots$ and $y_1, y_2, \ldots$. Two of the keys x_i and y_i then are used to find a shared secret s via Diffie-Hellman key exchange (DH). From s two keys for AES encryption and Message Authentication Code

(MAC) are derived. Messages then are encrypted using AES. Authentication is ensured with MAC. Each time a message is sent, a new key x_{i+1} or y_{i+1} is generated, a new secret s' is calculated and the old key deleted.

Silent Circle Instant Messaging Protocol (SCIMP) [11] is another end-to-end encrypted IM protocol, which ensures perfect forward secrecy and message authentication. A sender X generates an Elliptic Curve Diffie-Hellman (ECDH) key pair and sends a hash commitment to the receiver Y. Then, Y generates another ECDH key pair and sends a hash commitment to X. X checks, whether the shared secret and the commitment match, and the validity of the public key of Y. Then, X calculates a master and session key and sends another message, containing a MAC to Y. Similarly, Y checks, whether the shared secrets match and the public key of X is valid. Now Y can calculate the same master and session keys. Y then verifies the confirmation code and sends a confirmation code itself. Afterward, messages can be exchanged using AES encryption. New keys are derived by a hash-based key derivation function for every message using the last key, which then is deleted.

In [8] another secure IM protocol is described. It uses a modified DH to find a common key within a group of users. The initiator of a new communication generates a random number and computes a message from it. The message is sent to the server. The server modifies it, such that every new participant can perform DH with the public key of the initiator. This allows, to get a common shared secret within a group of participants. To achieve this, the server generates a unique secret $a_i \in \mathbb{Z}_q$ for each user u_i at the registration procedure. This secret is fixed by a certificate $g^{a_i} \bmod p$, which is sent to the u_i. This certificate is accepted by sending $g^{x_i a_i} \bmod p$ to the server, where $x_i \in \mathbb{Z}_q$ is a random secret. User u_i gets a common key with user u_j by, first, picking a random $r \in \mathbb{Z}_q$ and sending $z = g^r \bmod p$ to the server. The server calculates $b_j = z^{a_j} \bmod p$ and sends it to u_j. u_i calculates $k = h(y_j^r \bmod p)$, where $y_j = g^{x_j a_j}$ is the public key of u_j. u_j gets the same key k by computing $k = h(b_j^{x_j} \bmod p) = h(g^{r a_j x_j} \bmod p)$. p and q are secure primes, such that $q | p - 1$ and $\mathbb{Z}_p^*$ is a multiplicative group of order q. The common key then is used for symmetric encryption.

Another secure IM protocol is described in [20]. It is based on elliptic curve cryptography and uses three phases: registration, client-server communication, and client-client communication. In the registration phase, a public key point $y_S = x_S \bullet G$ is used by the server. x_S is a randomly selected large integer and G is the base point. A client generates a random secret x_A and a public key $y_A = x_A \bullet G$. It further calculates a master key $K_A = x_A \bullet y_S$. y_A is sent to the server. The server calculates the same master key through $K_A = x_S \bullet y_A$. Using K_A, a random string R_S is encrypted together with a hash of the previously received message. This is sent to the client, which decrypts it and compares the hash of its own sent message with the one it received from the server. Then, R_S is signed by the client and sent to the server. Using the established master key K_A between client and server they can find a session key K_{AS}. The user generates a symmetric key K_{AS}, encrypts it, using K_A, and sends it to the server. The server generates a random string R_S and again, calculates a hash of the previously received message. Both parts are encrypted, using K_A and sent to the client. The client decrypts the message, compares the hash values, and encrypts a hash value of the whole message, using K_{AS}. For the communication between two clients A and B, they receive each other's public key from the server. Both generate random integers x_A, and x_B and calculate $G_A = x_A \bullet G$ and $G_B = x_B \bullet G$. Both messages are signed and sent to the other client. After signature verification the clients use ECDH to calculate the common point $K_{AB} = x_A \bullet G_B = x_B \bullet G_A$ which then is used to encrypt messages between A and B.

The *Signal* protocol [10] uses a system called double ratchet to manage common keys between two peers. It uses key chains for sending and receiving, where each key is used as an input for a new key. Both sending and receiving chains are derived from a root chain. The root chain itself has a DH ratchet as an input. Sent or received messages are used for the key derivation in the corresponding chain. The inputs for this ratchet are renewed as often as possible: when a client sends a message, it always includes key material for a key exchange. When the client receives key material it calculates a new key on the ratchet. Further, a new key on the root chain is derived from it. Additionally, it is used as an input for new keys on the sending and receiving chains. The Signal protocol is used in variations in other protocols, like *OMEMO* [15] or *WhatsApp* [3].

Threema [16] is another system for end-to-end encrypted messages. Each user creates a key pair for EC cryptography. Public keys are stored on the server. Three different verification levels for keys exist. On the lowest level keys are not verified. On the next level, a matching phone number or email address is found. By scanning a 2D code from the mobile phone of a peer, a key can be verified for the highest level. Two peers can find a shared key by using DH. Messages are encrypted using a random nonce and the shared key using the XSalsa20 stream cipher. With Poly1305 a MAC is calculated for an encrypted message. MAC, ciphertext, and nonce are sent together. Messages for groups of more than two peers are encrypted for each peer individually, except for larger files, like images, videos, or audio. These are encrypted using a random symmetric key and uploaded to the server, the key is encrypted using the keys within the group.

Pretty Good Privacy (PGP) [5] and *S/MIME* [13] are two protocols for the encryption of emails. Both protocols use public-key cryptography to encrypt a symmetric key, which is used to encrypt the contents of the emails. The public keys are used for signatures, as well. This allows, to encrypt the contents once, whereas the symmetric key is encrypted for each recipient of the email. In both protocols, a symmetric key is used for the whole conversation, which may contain multiple emails and answers from different participants. PGP uses a trust system, whereas in S/MIME a system using X.509 certificates is used. *FlyByNight* [9] is a protocol to ensure privacy within Facebook. It uses JavaScript for client-side encryption. All sensitive messages are encrypted before sending them to the server. Keys are managed by the Facebook interfaces, but users need an additional password for flyByNight. Messages between users are encrypted using the public keys of the recipients. Proxy cryptography is used, whenever messages or information is shared between multiple users. For proxy cryptography, each participant has multiple keys. With one key, the information is encrypted once and then stored on the server. When a participant wants to access the information the server uses the proxy key to modify the encrypted information. Then, the participant can use the third key to decrypt it.

In [14] another system for end-to-end encryption of messages is proposed. The system works in web browsers, running JavaScript. Comparable to S/MIME and PGP, public keys of peers are used to encrypt symmetric keys for conversations. The symmetric keys are used to encrypt messages between two or multiple participants. All messages are signed, using another key. Public keys can be verified by users comparable to Threema by exchanging QR codes.

A scheme for quorum controlled asymmetric proxy re-encryption is presented in [7]. In the scheme, the server modifies ciphertexts using verifiable translation certificates. In contrast to our approach, the ciphertexts are re-encrypted especially for a specific user, using transformations defined by the user. Therefore, access cannot be revoked in the scheme, in contrast to our approach.

An approach to reduce the amount of re-keying messages when users join or leave encrypted groups is presented in [18]. Here, a directed acyclic graph is constructed. This graph contains u-nodes for users and k-nodes for keys. Each u-node has outgoing edges to at least one k-node. k-nodes have one or more incoming edge and can have none, one, or more outgoing edges. When users join or leave a group, new keys are distributed to all users of the group and all parent k-nodes and their parents. The amount of these messages is reduced because some of the keys can be sent to the parent groups of users. E.g. in a tree containing six u-nodes $u_0, u_1, \ldots u_5$, where the first three nodes are in a group g_1 and connected to k_1 and the others are in g_2 and connected to k_2. Both k-nodes are in g_0 and connected to k_0. When user u_6 joins g_1 the keys k_1 and k_0 are updated to k_1' and k_0'. u_6 receives keys k_0' and k_1'. The old group g_1 receives k_1' and the old group g_0 receives k_0', instead of sending them to all members individually. In contrast to our scheme, all prior messages to a joining (leaving) member have to be re-encrypted, when access should be possible (revoked).

3   Background and Model

A message board is a collection of topics. A topic can consist of different messages. Each message can have answers or comments by the same or other users. Some message boards allow having topics inside topics. In contrast to online chats, most message boards are not used for live interaction between users. Messages are written and can be answered or commented on later. Often, those messages are long, when compared to messages of online chats. They can contain images or files. Message boards can contain public and private topics. Any user may read or write messages in public topics, whereas in private topics the contents are protected and can only be read by persons with granted access. Message boards not only can contain messages with answers and comments, but interactive maps with annotations, surveys and polls, link collections, wiki pages, blogs, and files.

3.1   Background

For a better understanding, in the following a user u, is a general user of an OSN. If a user is allowed to access the private content of the message board he is called a participant. Whereas, if the user is not allowed he is called non-participant. An administrator in the following is a special participant, who has privileged rights. An administrator can delete, modify, or move content, as well as, change access rights, re-encrypt content, or change the quorum. A quorum is a set of participants and administrators, called members. The term head of content is used for the first stored content in a content chain. I.e. a new topic with a question is the head, every answer to this topic is in the content chain. This means, that beginning from the first content a chain of subsequent content is constructed, allowing to retrieve content one part after another. A content chain can contain a single topic, or multiple topics, or even a sub-message board. $h(x)$ is a secure key derivation function like PBKDF2, or another secure hashing function. The function calculates a value $y = h(x)$, such that calculating x from y is computationally infeasible. The term $h^{[n]}(x)$ denotes that the function $h(x)$ is applied n times, e.g. $h^{[3]}(x) = h(h(h(x)))$. Note, that h(x) itself can use key stretching methods, like multiple iterations. Private content in the message board is encrypted using the homomorphic encryption scheme of Elgamal [2]. In the scheme, a ciphertext of a message m can be computed by a sender A in the following way: A choses a number r uniformly between 0 and $p-1$, where p is a large prime and $p-1$ has at least one large prime factor. Then A computes $c_1 \equiv g^{x_B r} \cdot m \mod p$, and $c_0 \equiv g^r \mod p$ where g is a public value, known to A and B and $g^{x_B} \mod p$ is the public key of B. The ciphertext then is the tuple (c_0, c_1). B can decrypt m by first, computing $g^{x_B r} \equiv c_0^{x_B} \mod p$ and second, computing $\frac{c_1}{g^{x_B r}} \equiv \frac{g^{x_B r} \cdot m}{g^{x_B r}} \equiv m \mod p$. The security of the Elgamal encryption scheme is related to the Decisional Diffie-Hellman Problem [1]. Given a cyclic group $\mathbb{G}$ of finite order q, with generator g and $a, b, c \in \mathbb{Z}_q$ are randomly chosen. Then there exist no efficient algorithm, which can distinguish between the two distributions $\langle g^a, g^b, g^{ab} \rangle$ and $\langle g^a, g^b, g^c \rangle$. For the Elgamal encryption this implies, that given g^a and g^b the key g^{ab} cannot be distinguished from a random group element. Therefore, the encryption $g^{ab} \cdot m$ of m cannot be distinguished from a random group element. In the following all operations using the Elgamal scheme are calculated modulo p, where p meets the requirements for secure Elgamal encryption.

3.2   Model

We assume a Client-Server Model, where all users of the OSN connect to the server. The server stores all necessary data, including the webpages containing the message board. Every user owns a key pair for public-key encryption and signatures. The public keys of users are exchanged through the server and can be verified in a way comparable to Threema, where users verify their keys in person. Therefore, we assume that all public keys are verified. This allows, for example, to safely exchange a key via Diffie-Hellman without further measures.

Additionally, all messages are signed and the correct senders are ensured. In this model, the message board is a tree-like structure, where each node is either, a sub-message board, a collection of topics, or a topic. Each topic can be a leaf node if no message was appended to the topic. I.e. no answer or comment to a message was posted. If one or more messages to a topic exist, these are child nodes and connected to the topic node without any branches. Every node can be the head of a content chain. When such a node is not public, all child nodes are private, as well.

3.3   Private Content and Quorums

Private content is end-to-end encrypted. All participants, that know a key of a node in the content chain can derive the next key via a key derivation function or a secure hash function. This allows accessing all content, starting from the head of content serially, when access to the head of content was granted. Further, this allows a user to get access to a node within the content chain, such that all following messages, topics, and sub-message boards can be accessed. The parent nodes remain encrypted and therefore inaccessible. Each participant can derive the next key from the last known key. Therefore, it is easy to append new messages to the content chain. As the derivation function is the same for all participants, any other participant then can decrypt appended messages without further measures. To access the private content, a user has to ask a quorum for permission. A quorum is a group of participants with special rights. The quorum is determined by the administrator and can contain one or many members. They can have access to the encrypted content, but this is not necessary. On the other hand, a participant with access is not necessarily a member of the quorum. Quorum participants are users selected by the administrator whom he believes to be trustworthy. They are trustworthy enough, such that the administrator grants them access to the private keys of the content. Every user asking for access to the private content then has to ask the single quorum member. Whenever this member cannot answer, the access is denied, until the member answers. Every member of the quorum has to receive the private keys for the encrypted content from another member. Additionally, the administrator chooses a counter value c and encrypts it as c_1, using the scheme of Elgamal. The server delivers c_1 to each user asking for the content. Every quorum member who is asked for access by the user then reduces this value, until it reaches zero. Then the last quorum member can decrypt the content for the user. The encryption paramenters for c_1 are shared within the quorum. The counter value should be smaller than the size of the quorum. This leads to the fact, that a user does not have to ask every member for access, but only some of them.

4   Proposed Protocols

The following protocols allow storing encrypted content on a server. They enable symmetric or asymmetric encryption. This allows to choose the appropriate protocols for different scenarios, where small or large contents are exchanged, and the speed of encryption and decryption matters or is negligible. Note that the cal-culations in the protocols are modulo p, where p meets the properties required for secure Elgamal encryption (see Sect. 3.1). The additional mod p will be omitted for brevity.

4.1   Content Chain

Content has to be organized in a tree-like structure. Every node can be the start of a content chain. At every node branches are allowed. This means, that a node n has more than one child. When a user has access to n it can access all other branches, as well. In a message board, the tree-like structure is given: Every sub-message board allows to branch. Each new topic, then, is the start of a branch. In other applications, comparable, the creation time can be used to construct a path, branches can be created by the given content. The content chain contains not only content in plaintext. Private content is encrypted and sent to the server as ciphertext. The server stores the encrypted content. For every user access-ing the content, it generates additional encryption parameters. This allows the server to deliver a unique version of the encrypted content to every user. This works by encrypting the content using the scheme of Elgamal. However, in the symmetric version of the proposed protocols the content is encrypted using AES and then stored on the server. Here, only the keys are encrypted using the asym-metric protocol of Elgamal. Therefore, only the keys are encrypted using unique encryption parameters per user, not the content. An example of a content chain is displayed in Fig. 1.

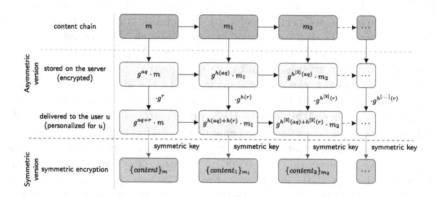

Fig. 1. A private content chain. In the symmetric version the actual content $m, m_1, \ldots$ is never delivered to the server. Instead, for every m_n a ciphertext is stored on the server. The server generates an additional random parameter r for a user. Using r, the encrypted content is modified, such that different users receive different versions. In the symmetric version m_i is not the content, but a key for a symmetric encryption of the content $\{content_i\}_{m_i}$.

4.2 Accessing Private Content

Each head of private content m is stored on the server as a ciphertext $g^{aq} \cdot m$. A user that wants to access the data sends a request to the server. The server first checks, whether the respective user has non-revoked access to the contents. In this case, the precomputed and stored values are sent. If the user is not allowed to access the content chain the server aborts. Otherwise, a tuple $(t_{pk}, t_{ctr}, t_{rnd}, t_c)$ is calculated by the server. $t_{pk} = g^s$, where s is a unique random number serves as a public key. The second value $t_{rnd} = (g^a)^s \cdot r$ contains another unique random number r and the public key g^a, where a is the private key of the head of content. a is selected by the adminstrator, when the head of content is created. The administrator has to provided a to all quorum members. The third value is $t_{ctr} = g^{a+sr} \cdot c_1 \cdot h(r + c_1)$. It is calculated, using the counter value c_1 of the quorum, the public key g^a, and both random values r and s. The actual content is in $t_c = g^{aq+r} \cdot m$. It is calculated by the server as $t_c = g^{aq} \cdot m \cdot g^r$. The values s and r are stored for the next access of the user. The user sends the first three values t_{pk}, t_{ctr}, and t_{rnd} of the tuple t to the first member of the quorum. If access to the content has to be granted the member calculates $r = (t_{pk})^{-a} \cdot t_{rnd} = g^{-as} \cdot g^{as} \cdot r$, where a is the private key for the content. Then, the member calculates $c_1 \cdot h(r + c_1) = t_{ctr} \cdot g^{-a} \cdot (t_{pk})^{-r}$ and tries different values c_1' until $c_1 \cdot h(r + c_1) = c_1' \cdot h(r + c_1')$ is satisfied. The counter value $c = c_1 = c_1'$, then, is compared to the access restrictions. If $c = 0$, the member answers $(g^{-(aq+r)}, h(aq), h(r))$, where $h(x)$ is a secure key derivation function or hash function. $g^{-(aq+r)}$ can be calculated from the public value g^{aq} and r. If $c > 0$, A new unique value s' is randomly chosen by the member. Then, $c_2 = c-1$ is calculated and encrypted by the member as $t_{ctr}' = g^{a+s'r} \cdot c_2 \cdot h(r+c_2)$. Further, $t_{pk}' = g^{s'}$ and $t_{rnd}' = (g^a)^{s'} \cdot r$ are calculated. The member sends $(t_{pk}', t_{ctr}', t_{rnd}')$ back to the user. Based on the response of the member, the user either can decrypt the content or he has to send the tuple to another member. To decrypt the content the user calculates $m = t_c \cdot g^{-(aq+r)} \cdot m = g^{aq+r} \cdot g^{-(aq+r)} \cdot m$. The values $h(aq), h(r)$ are known, because the user received them from the last quorum member. They can be used to access the other private content of the content chain. If $m_1, m_2, \ldots, m_n$ is the following private content in the chain, it is encrypted using the keys $h(g^{aq}), h^{[2]}(g^{aq}), \ldots, h^{[n]}(g^{aq})$. The server chooses the encryption parameters as $h(r), h^{[2]}(r), \ldots, h^{[n]}(r)$, as long as access for the user was not revoked by a quorum member. The procedure to access private content is displayed in Algorithm 1 and Algorithm 2.

The proposed algorithms may not be suitable for all usages, as public-key cryptography is not as fast as symmetric cryptography (see Sect. 4.4 for comparisons). Therefore, the protocols may be used for short messages, only. With slight modifications, the protocols can be used together with symmetric encryption, like AES. The changes are the following: 1) The encrypted components $m, m_1, m_2, \ldots, m_n$ are keys used for symmetric encryption of the content $content, content_1, content_2, \ldots, content_n$. 2) In Algorithm 1, Step 3b the server has to store the value $h(r)$ for the user as an authentication code. Therefore, in Step 4 the user has to send $h(r)$, which he gets from the quorum. In Step 5, the server then checks, whether $h(r)$ is the correct authentication code. In Step 4.2, additionally the server has to send $\{content_i\}_{m_i}$. The user then decrypts $content_i$ in Step 9, after calculating the key m_i. For Protocol 2 no modifications are needed. The modifications in the following are called symmetric versions. The symmetric version is an extension to the asymmetric version.

Algorithm 1. The user wants to access the private content chain, starting at $g^{aq} \cdot m$. The calculations of Step 9 are possible when the user received the message in Step 4a of Algorithm 2, from the quorum.

User u	**Server** (knows g, g^a, $g^{aq} \cdot m$, c_1)
1. wants to access m, sends id_m	
2.	checks if there is access for u
If access is forbidden:	
3a.	sends error message, terminates
If there is no access:	
3b.	chooses random r, s
	stores r, s for u
Else:	
3c.	takes stored values r, s
	calculates $t_{pk} = g^s$
	calculates $t_{ctr} = g^{a+sr} \cdot c_1 \cdot h(r + c_1)$
	calculates $t_{rnd} = (g^a)^s \cdot r$
	calculates $t_c = g^{aq+r} \cdot m$
	sends $t = (t_{pk}, t_{ctr}, t_{rnd}, t_c)$
	$\vdots$
4. wants to access m_i, sends id_{m_i}	
5.	takes stored value r
	calculates $t_{m_i} = g^{h^{[i]}(aq) + h^{[i]}(r)} \cdot m_i$
	sends t_{m_i}
9. calculates $m_i = t_{m_i} \cdot g^{-(h^{[i]}(aq) + h^{[i]}(r))}$	
	$\vdots$

4.3   Changing Access

The additional encryption parameter r allows the administrators to quickly change the encryption of the stored content. Further, access for different users is easy to manage with the proposed protocols.

Granting and Revoking Access. To allow a user to access the content is easy. The user ID is sent to the server and all quorum members. When the user wants to access the content it contacts the server and the quorum, like described in Protocols 1 and 2. For the revocation of access the user ID is sent to the server and the quorum. Then, every quorum member knows that requests of

---

Algorithm 2. The user wants to access private content. Tuple t is received from the server. The values $(t_{pk}, t_{ctr}, t_{rnd})$ are sent to the quorum members. They can check with the decrypted counter value, whether enough members granted access. A quorum member provides either another tuple, that has to be sent to another quorum member, or a tuple, which allows decrypting the content.

User	**Quorum member** (knows g, a, q, and encryption parameters for counter values)
1. sends $(t_{pk}, t_{ctr}, t_{rnd})$	
2.	calculates $r = t_{rnd} \cdot (t_{pk})^{-a} = g^{as} \cdot g^{-as} \cdot r$
	calculates $c_1 \cdot h(r + c_1) = t_{ctr} \cdot g^{-a} \cdot (t_{pk})^{-r}$
	tries different values c_1' until the equation
	$c_1 \cdot h(r + c_1) = c_1' \cdot h(r + c_1')$ is satisfied
	sets $c = c_1'$
If $c = 0$:	
3a.	calculates $t' = (g^{-(aq+r)}, h(r), h(aq))$
	sends t'
4a. calculates m as	
$m = g^{-(aq+r)} \cdot g^{(aq+r)} \cdot m$	
Else:	
3b.	sets $c' = c - 1$, encrypts it as c_2 using the same parameters, chooses random s'
	calculates $t_{pk}' = g^{s'}$
	calculates $t_{ctr}' = g^{a+s'r} \cdot c_2 \cdot h(r + c_2)$
	calculates $t_{rnd}' = (g^a)^{s'} \cdot r$
	sends $t' = (t_{pk}', t_{ctr}', t_{rnd}')$
4b. sends t' to the next member	

---

the user can be ignored. The server deletes the parameters r and s for the user. This prevents the server from being able to compute the same encrypted content again. Knowledge of the user about the decryption keys then is worthless. In the symmetric version, the authentication code $h(r)$ for the user is deleted, as well.

Removing Encryption. Private contents can be made public by publishing the encryption parameters. The administrator sends a and q to the server. The server can forward them to all users that want to access the content chain.

Encrypting Public Contents. Public content can be stored in two ways on the server. Either, it is not encrypted or the necessary keys are published. In the first case, content is stored as m, in the second case, it is stored as $m' = g^{aq} \cdot m$, where g^a is the public key and q is an encryption parameter. By multiplying m or m' with some g^b it can be encrypted or re-encrypted. The problem is that knowledge of g^b undermines the encryption. Therefore, public content should be removed from the server and stored again as encrypted ciphertexts.

Re-encryption of Contents. Re-encryption of encrypted content is possible in contrast to the encryption of public contents. All content in the content chain can be multiplied with another secure random parameter b. A user u with knowledge of the previous decryption keys $g^{-(aq+r)}$, $h(r)$, and $h(aq)$ can compute $m_i \cdot b$ from $g^{h^{[i]}(aq)h^{[i]}(r)} \cdot m_i \cdot b$. m_i can only be computed by u if b is known. In the symmetric protocol, the keys can be re-encrypted using the same procedure. To modify a ciphertext $\{content_i\}_{m_i}$, such that a new key m_i' instead of m_i is used, the fraction $\Delta = \{content_i\}_{m_i'}/\{content_i\}_{m_i}$, of both ciphertexts can be computed and sent to the server. The server does not know anything about m or m_i. Thus, it cannot compute $content_i$ from the information it knows.

4.4   Performance

To asses the performance of the discussed approach, some tests were performed. For the tests, a laptop with an Intel® Core™ i7-8550U CPU and 16 GB of RAM was used. Because the message board is a web application two encryptions using JavaScript were implemented. Using the jsbn library [19] procedures were written to encrypt and decrypt messages of different sizes using Elgamal. As a comparison, the AES-256 encryption and decryption procedures of the Webcrypto API [17] were used to encrypt messages of the same sizes. The messages were 512, 1024, 1536 and 2048 bits long. The primes for the Elgamal groups had lengths of 1072, 1543 and 2051 bits. As expected, AES always performed better, especially with longer messages. For smaller messages and the smallest prime, the run-time of encryption was on average below 800 ms and for decryption, it was below 650 ms. These values are acceptable and can be used in the context of OSNs, where interaction can be asynchronous. The run-times are displayed in Table 1.

Table 1. Encryption and decryption run-times with AES-256 and Elgamal.

Message length	AES-256		Elgamal		
	Encryption	Decryption	Prime length	Encryption	Decryption
512 bit	23.6 ms	13.9 ms	1072 bit	796.4 ms	599.4 ms
1024 bit	22.7 ms	17.0 ms	1072 bit	720.0 ms	627.8 ms
1536 bit	26.1 ms	15.3 ms	1543 bit	1357.4 ms	1832.3 ms
2048 bit	28.9 ms	23.3 ms	2051 bit	3452.3 ms	4425.9 ms

5   Security Analysis

The security of the presented protocols relies on the security of Elgamal. In the following, different scenarios on how users or the server could try to read encrypted private content are discussed.

5.1   The Server Cannot Access Private Content

In the asymmetric version, the server receives the following data from administrators and users for a content chain: The public key g^a, the encrypted counter value c_1, the encrypted content $g^{aq} \cdot m, g^{h(aq)} \cdot m_1, \ldots, g^{h^{[n]}}(aq) \cdot m_n$, and requests, containing the ID of the data $id_m, id_{m_1}, \ldots, id_{m_n}$. Using IDs or encrypted counter values, no knowledge about the content is gained. In fact, IDs and the quorum requirements may be known by any user. Using g^a and any encrypted content, e.g. $g^{aq} \cdot m$ no knowledge can be gained. From any two ciphertexts, e.g. $g^{aq} \cdot m$ and $g^{h(aq)} \cdot m_1$ the server is not able to compute m or m_1.

The content is saved as ciphertexts $\{content\}_m, \{content_1\}_{m_1}, \ldots,$ $\{content_n\}_{m_n}$ in the symmetric version. The corresponding keys $m, m_1, \ldots, m_n$ are not known to the server. As the server is not able to compute any m in the asymmetric model, it is not possible for the server to decrypt any content, when a secure symmetric encryption scheme is used.

5.2   Received Tuples Do Not Break the Encryption

A user u receives different tuples from the server: $t_{init} = (t_{pk}, t_{ctr}, t_{rnd}, t_c)$ and $t_{c_i} = (g^{h^{[i]}(aq)})^{h^{[i]}(r)} \cdot m_i$. From the quorum members u receives different $t^n = (t_{pk}^n, t_{ctr}^n, t_{rnd}^n)$ and $t_{success} = (g^{-(aq+r)}, h(r), h(aq))$. The tuples t_{init} and t^n have the same structure, except for the last component, which is not present in the tuples t^n. The components are: $t_{pk} = g^s$, $t_{ctr} = g^{a+sr} \cdot c_1 \cdot h(r + c_1)$, $t_{rnd} = (g^a)^s \cdot r$, and $t_c = g^{aq+r} \cdot m$. For these tuples, any user receives different components, because all $r, r', r'', \ldots$ and $s, s', s'', \ldots$ are drawn uniquely at random per user. Therefore, knowing multiple of these tuples gives no exploitable advantage. The tuple $t_{success}$, of course, allows u to compute any m or m_i from t_c and t_{c_i}, respectively. Knowledge of m allows u to compute g^{aq+r} from t_c, but as no other component uses the same factor, u gains no additional knowledge. The same holds for m_i and t_{c_i}. Knowledge of $h(r)$ and $h(aq)$ allows u to compute any m_i, but as $h(x)$ meets the requirements of a cryptographic hash function, it is infeasible to calculate r or aq. Therefore, u cannot use the tuples to exploit the asymmetric protocols and gain access to any additional content.

Regarding the symmetric protocols, the same arguments hold. Additionally, any two contents $\{content_i\}_{m_i}$ and $\{content_j\}_{m_j}$ are encrypted with different keys $m_i \neq m_j$. Knowledge of one key, i.e. m_i does not allow to decrypt another ciphertext where another key was used.

5.3   No Access with Colluding Users

In the asymmetric version, two users u and u' receive two different initial tuples $t = (t_{pk}, t_{ctr}, t_{rnd}, t_c)$ and $t' = (t'_{pk}, t'_{ctr}, t'_{rnd}, t'_c)$ from the server. These tuples differ at every component. The server uses two random numbers r, s for u, whereas, for u' the numbers r' and s' are independently chosen. This results in the following distinctions: $t_{pk} = g^s$ for u and $t'_{pk} = g^{s'}$ for u' where g is public and s, s' are not related. u receives $t_{ctr} = g^{a+sr} \cdot c_1 \cdot h(r + c_1)$, u' receives

$t'_{ctr} = g^{a+s'r'} \cdot c_1 \cdot h(r'+c_1)$. c_1 is an encrypted counter. Combining this knowledge eliminates this factor from the tuples, but g^{a+sr}, $h(r+c_1)$, $g^{a+s'r'}$ and $h(r'+c_1)$ are not determined by this. Finding the correct $h(r+c_1)$ or $h(r'+c_1)$, even with known c_1 means u and u' have to try all possible values for r or r'. The components $t_{rnd} = (g^a)^s \cdot r$ and $t'_{rnd} = (g^a)^{s'} \cdot r'$, again, have the non-related factors $(g^a)^s, (g^a)^{s'}$, and r, r'. The last components $t_c = g^{aq+r} \cdot m$ and $t'_c = g^{aq+r'} \cdot m$ have the common factor m, but again g^{aq+r} and $g^{aq+r'}$ are not related, because of the random factors r, r'. Therefore, users u and u' do not learn anything from combining their server tuples. All intermediate tuples from the quorum members have the same structure as the initial server tuples. They differ in the random encryption parameters r and s, and the counter value c_i. Therefore, their knowledge is not exploitable by u and u', as well. The last tuple from the quorum members is $(g^{-(aq+r)}, h(r), h(aq))$ for u and $(g^{-(aq+r')}, h(r'), h(aq))$ for u'. $h(aq)$ is the same for both u and u'. Again, $h(r)$ and $h(r')$ are two random numbers without any relation. The same statement holds for $g^{-(aq+r)}$ and $g^{-(aq+r')}$. Therefore, two users u and u' cannot collude and use their tuples to attack the protocol.

In the symmetric version, two users u and u' use the same symmetric key m_i for content $content_i$. Therefore, a user u can send the key to another user u'. The server stores different authentication codes $h(r)$ and $h(r')$ for the same content chain for users u and u'. These are not related and cannot be computed without knowledge of r and r'.

5.4   Removed User Has No Access

A user u that was removed from a content chain may have received all tuples from the server and from the quorum members. To gain access to content $content_i$, u has to send id_{m_i} to the server (see Protocol 1, Step 4). As the server already deleted r for u it cannot calculate t_{c_i} for u. This prevents u from accessing content in the asymmetric version.

In the symmetric protocol, in addition, the user has to send an authentication code $h(r)$, which cannot be verified by the server, because r and $h(r)$ were deleted. This prevents u from accessing the content in the symmetric protocol.

5.5   No Access Between Different Content Chains

Two content chains $chain = m, m_1, \ldots, m_n$ and $chain' = m', m'_1, \ldots, m'_o$ may be maintained by the same administrators and share the same quorum. Then, on the one hand, it is possible, that they share the same public key g^a. On the other hand, the additional encryption parameters, q and q' differ. Therefore, even if the content is the same, i.e. $m = m'$, the server receives two different ciphertexts $g^{aq} \cdot m \neq g^{aq'} \cdot m$. q, q' are uniformly chosen secure random numbers. This results in not related tuples from the server, between $chain$ and $chain'$. The tuples, sent by the quorum members are not related, as well. Therefore, having access to one content chain does not give access to another content chain, even if g^a is the same for different chains.

The same arguments hold for the symmetric protocols, as well.

6   Conclusion

In this work, we presented protocols for access management in end-to-end encrypted message boards for Online Social Networks. The protocols allow us to distribute keys and content and to revoke access to these contents. For applications where communication happens asynchronously or the content is small, like short text messages, the asymmetric protocols can be used. Additionally, we discussed extensions to the protocols to utilize the advantages of faster encryption and decryption in symmetric encryption protocols. This allows using the protocols whenever large amounts of data have to be encrypted, transmitted, and decrypted. The protocols are applicable for any type of content, that can be organized in a tree-like structure. This includes message boards, wikis, or groups that are used in different OSNs. We have shown that the protocols meet the necessary security requirements and cannot be exploited by the server or users, or by multiple colluding users. Further, access to the encrypted contents is managed by different quorums, where different trustworthy users have to accept the request of a user. This helps in mitigating the effect, that quorum members are not able to answer.

Yet, the most important limitation of our protocols lies in the fact that all quorum members need to know the encryption keys, which gives them the possibility to attack the protocols, like in not handing out the correct keys or even encrypting the contents again, with a new key. Therefore, further research has to be made, to utilize the properties of secret sharing schemes, such that no quorum member has to know all keys.

Acknowledgements. The authors acknowledge the financial support by the Federal Ministry of Education and Research of Germany in the framework of SoNaTe (project number 16SV7405).

References

1. Boneh, D.: The decision Diffie-Hellman problem. In: Buhler, J.P. (ed.) ANTS 1998. LNCS, vol. 1423, pp. 48–63. Springer, Heidelberg (1998). https://doi.org/10.1007/BFb0054851
2. Elgamal, T.: A public key cryptosystem and a signature scheme based on discrete logarithms. IEEE Trans. Inf. Theory **31**(4), 469–472 (1985)
3. Evans, J.: Whatsapp partners with open whispersystems to end-to-end encrypt billions of messages a day, November 2014. https://techcrunch.com/2014/11/18/end-to-end-for-everyone/
4. Facebook Inc.: Facebook Q3 2019 Results, October 2019. https://s21.q4cdn.com/399680738/files/doc_financials/2019/q3/Q3-2019-Earnings-Presentation.pdf
5. Finney, H., Donnerhacke, L., Callas, J., Thayer, R.L., Shaw, D.: OpenPGP Message Format. RFC 4880, November 2007. https://doi.org/10.17487/RFC4880. https://rfc-editor.org/rfc/rfc4880.txt
6. Hootsuite & We Are Social: Digital 2019 Q4 Global Digital Statshot (2019). https://datareportal.com/reports/digital-2019-q4-global-digital-statshot

7. Jakobsson, M.: On quorum controlled asymmetric proxy re-encryption. In: Imai, H., Zheng, Y. (eds.) PKC 1999. LNCS, vol. 1560, pp. 112–121. Springer, Heidelberg (1999). https://doi.org/10.1007/3-540-49162-7_9

8. Kikuchi, H., Tada, M., Nakanishi, S.: Secure instant messaging protocol preserving confidentiality against administrator. In: 2014 18th International Conference on Advanced Information Networking and Applications (AINA 2004), vol. 2, pp. 27–30. IEEE (2004)

9. Lucas, M.M., Borisov, N.: FlyByNight: mitigating the privacy risks of social networking. In: Proceedings of the 7th ACM Workshop on Privacy in the Electronic Society (WPES 2008), pp. 1–8. ACM, New York (2008). https://doi.org/10.1145/1456403.1456405. http://doi.acm.org/10.1145/1456403.1456405

10. Marlinspike, M.: The Double Ratchet Algorithm, November 2016. https://signal.org/docs/specifications/doubleratchet/

11. Moscaritolo, V., Belvin, G., Zimmermann, P.: Silent Circle Instant Messaging Protocol - Protocol Specification, December 2012. https://web.archive.org/web/20150402122917/silentcircle.com/sites/default/themes/silentcircle/assets/downloads/SCIMP_paper.pdf

12. OTR Development Team: Off-the-Record Messaging Protocol version 3 (2012). https://otr.cypherpunks.ca/Protocol-v3-4.1.1.html

13. Schaad, J., Ramsdell, B., Turner, S.: Secure/Multipurpose Internet Mail Extensions (S/MIME) Version 4.0 Message Specification. RFC 8551, April 2019. https://doi.org/10.17487/RFC8551. https://rfc-editor.org/rfc/rfc8551.txt

14. Schillinger, F., Schindelhauer, C.: End-to-end encryption schemes for online social networks. In: Wang, G., Feng, J., Bhuiyan, M.Z.A., Lu, R. (eds.) SpaCCS 2019. LNCS, vol. 11611, pp. 133–146. Springer, Cham (2019). https://doi.org/10.1007/978-3-030-24907-6_11

15. Straub, A.: XEP-0384: OMEMO encryption (1999–2018). https://xmpp.org/extensions/xep-0384.html

16. Threema: Threema Cryptography Whitepaper, January 2019. https://threema.ch/press-files/cryptography_whitepaper.pdf

17. Web Cryptography API - W3C Recommendation 26 January 2017, January 2017. https://www.w3.org/TR/2017/REC-WebCryptoAPI-20170126/

18. Wong, C.K., Gouda, M., Lam, S.S.: Secure group communications using key graphs. IEEE/ACM Trans. Netw. 8(1), 16–30 (2000)

19. Wu, T.: JSBN library, September 2009. http://www-cs-students.stanford.edu/~tjw/jsbn/

20. Yang, C.H., Kuo, T.Y., Ahn, T., Lee, C.P.: Design and implementation of a secure instant messaging service based on elliptic-curve cryptography. J. Comput. 18(4), 31–38 (2008)

Establishing Secure Communication Channels Using Remote Attestation with TPM 2.0

Paul Georg Wagner[1](✉), Pascal Birnstill[2], and Jürgen Beyerer[1,2]

[1] Karlsruhe Institute of Technology, Karlsruhe, Germany
paul.wagner@kit.edu
[2] Fraunhofer Institute of Optronics, System Technologies and Image Exploitation IOSB, Karlsruhe, Germany

Abstract. Remote attestation allows a verifier to remotely check the integrity of a trusted computing platform. In recent years a number of attestation protocols based on Trusted Platform Modules (TPMs) have been proposed. These protocols cryptographically verify a trusted platform's state by exchanging TPM-signed quotes. Some of them also establish an encrypted channel to the trusted platform, which allows the verifier to transmit information that only the attested software stack can read. However, many existing attestation protocols are either vulnerable against man-in-the-middle attacks, or depend on outdated TPM specifications. In this work we analyze a recently developed attestation protocol that is being actively used to interconnect highly distributed trusted applications. We find this protocol to be vulnerable against a variant of the classical relay attack. In response to this threat we develop a lightweight remote attestation protocol based on the TPM 2.0 specification that is not vulnerable to this attack. Unlike previous proposals, our protocol relies solely on the TPM to establish a shared key on the attested channel, which significantly reduces its attack surface. Our protocol supports mutual attestation, perfect forward secrecy and is independent of the underlying network stack. We provide a reference implementation of our protocol and compare its performance to previous proposals. We also analyze its security properties using the Tamarin theorem prover.

Keywords: Trusted computing · Trusted Platform Modules · Remote attestation · Key establishment · Secure channels · Attestation protocols

1 Introduction

Trusted Platform Modules (TPMs) are tamper-resistant hardware chips that extend computer systems with basic security related features. Similar in nature to smart cards, TPMs provide a hardware implementation of cryptographic functions and protected storage for cryptographic keys. Since they are included in many motherboards, TPMs are arguably the most prevalent trusted computing

© Springer Nature Switzerland AG 2020
K. Markantonakis and M. Petrocchi (Eds.): STM 2020, LNCS 12386, pp. 73–89, 2020.
https://doi.org/10.1007/978-3-030-59817-4_5

technology today. One of the most interesting TPM capabilities is the remote verification of a trusted platform's software stack. For this the TPM uses volatile platform configuration registers (PCRs) to measure the current hardware and software configuration as an unforgeable fingerprint. A remote verifier can then request proof of the platform configuration in form of a quote that has been signed by the TPM. This quote contains a nonce generated by the verifier as well as the trusted platform's fingerprint, thereby attesting to the trusted software stack. After comparing the fingerprint to expected values, the verifier is convinced that the trusted platform indeed runs a legitimate software stack. Remote attestation protocols define how the verification of a trusted platform should be conducted over the network. Besides creating and transmitting TPM-signed quotes, most protocols also establish encrypted channels between the attested endpoints. Even though this has been a topic of comprehensive research in the past, currently there are very few ready-to-use protocol implementations available. One of the few actively used remote attestation protocols is the *Industrial Data Space Communication Protocol (IDSCP)* [10]. Introduced by Lux and Brost in 2018, IDSCP has been developed specifically for the Fraunhofer Industrial Data Space (IDS) project [12], which provides secure virtual data spaces for smart business ecosystems. The IDSCP protocol incorporates the benefits of several earlier proposals, such as TLS integration as well as support for mutual attestation and perfect forward secrecy. Also its code is publicly available on Github[1]. Because of these advantages, IDSCP is currently one of the most advanced attestation protocol in productive use.

In this work we present an attack on the IDSCP protocol in scenarios where multiple software components are providing an attestation endpoint on the trusted platform. This scenario is especially relevant in applications where we cannot predict what software will be considered trustworthy, but it applies to other use cases as well. In response to this threat we also develop a lightweight remote attestation protocol based on TPM 2.0 that is not vulnerable to this attack, while still keeping the advantages of IDSCP over previous proposals. Our protocol is easy to implement, supports mutual attestation and forward secrecy, and is independent of the used network stack. In addition our protocol keeps the secret parts of the shared keys used to encrypt the attested channel inside the TPM at all times, which is a security advantage over previous proposals. A reference implementation of our protocol as well as the formal model used for security verification are publicly available[2]. The remainder of this paper is structured as follows. In Sect. 2 we discuss the strengths and weaknesses of existing remote attestation protocols, before briefly presenting IDSCP and the vulnerabilities we found with it. In Sect. 3 we describe the design of our protocol and its reference implementation. Finally, in Sect. 4 we evaluate the proposed protocol in terms of functionality and security. We also verify the resilience of our protocol against the presented attack using the Tamarin theorem prover [11].

---

[1] https://github.com/industrial-data-space.
[2] https://gitlab-ext.iosb.fraunhofer.de/wagner/tpm20-attestation-protocol.

2   Discussion of Existing Protocols

In this section we first define requirements that attestation protocols should adhere to. Then we discuss the most important remote attestation protocols that have been proposed so far and point out their strengths and weaknesses. Finally we present a still unpublished attack on IDSCP.

2.1   Protocol Requirements

We define three *security requirements* S1 to S3 for remote attestation protocols.

(S1) Authentication: The protocol verifier unambiguously identifies and authenticates the attested platform. No attacker may forge the authentication.

(S2) Platform integrity verification: The protocol verifier is convinced that the attested platform runs a certain trusted software stack, i.e. its PCRs are set to specific values. No attacker is able to impersonate a trusted platform.

(S3) Secure key establishment: The protocol verifier establishes a shared secret with the attested platform. No attacker is able to determine this secret.

Any successful attack against the three main security requirements breaches the confidentiality and integrity of information transmitted over the secure channel. In order to represent security properties of the discussed protocols in finer detail, we distinguish four types of attacks with the additional requirements S4 to S7. Our attacker model consists of adversaries who control the network as well as any secret outside the TPM, including platform secrets such as TLS private keys.

(S4) No replay attacks: No attacker is able to break S1 to S3 by resending previously intercepted legitimate messages.

(S5) No insider attacks: No attacker with knowledge of platform secrets that are not protected by the TPM (e.g. TLS private keys) may break S1 to S3.

(S6) No relay attacks on protocol endpoint: No attacker is able to launch a relay attack targeting the specific protocol's attestation endpoint.

(S7) No relay attacks on non-protocol endpoint: No attacker is able to launch a relay attack targeting any other available attestation endpoint.

In addition to the security goals we define four *functional requirements* F1 to F4. They deal with protocol properties necessary to apply the solution to a wide range of dynamic and challenging tasks.

(F1) Mutual attestation: Establishing a secure channel through a single protocol handshake verifies the platform integrity of both peers.

(F2) Re-attestation: Any verifier can re-attest the trusted platform even after the protocol has established a shared secret.

(F3) Forward secrecy: Disclosing a long-term secret must not corrupt previously intercepted protocol sessions.

(F4) Protocol overhead: The attestation protocol must not generate substantial overhead in performance, implementation complexity and code base size.

2.2   Related Work

In recent years several remote attestation protocols have been proposed. However, most of them are not suitable for large-scale remote attestation applications, or have already been identified as vulnerable.

No Key Establishment or Attestation. Some protocols such as [5,13] only focus on conducting a remote attestation and do not include a shared key establishment (requirement S3). Since these attestation protocols cannot establish secure communication channels, they are unsuitable for scenarios where confidential information should be transmitted to a remote trusted software stack. A more recent project integrates the TPM 2.0 engine in OpenSSL[3]. However, this only allows OpenSSL to use the TPM hardware for its cryptographic operations, but does not provide a remotely attested secure channel (requirements S2 and S3).

Vulnerable Against Insider Attacks. Several protocols provide a secure channel between the verifier and the attested platform by combining remote attestation techniques with an underlying TLS protocol instance. When doing so it is vital to properly bind the keys responsible for creating the encrypted TLS channel to the attested trusted platform, because otherwise the protocols can become insecure. Cheng et al. [4] propose to establish the link between remote attestation and TLS by hashing the TLS pre-master secret into the quote. However, this approach is insecure against attackers with insider knowledge, such as administrators of attested systems. We have to assume that system administrators have access to long-term platform secrets, as long as they are not protected by the TPM. Hence they can simply use the TLS private keys to decrypt the pre-master secret that the legitimate trusted platform transmits during the TLS handshake. As a result, they can passively intercept secrets that an unsuspecting verifier sent across the trusted channel to the attested system. Remote attestation protocols susceptible to this kind of insider attack do not fulfill security requirement S5. Similarly Goldman et al. [7] attempt to link remote attestation with the SSL/TLS stack by adding an intermediate platform certificate signed by a trusted CA. This method also does not protect against insider attacks, because we have to assume that an insider attacker can obtain the unprotected private key corresponding to this new platform certificate. Zhou and Zhang [16] base their solution to this problem on pre-shared passwords. However, this approach is also vulnerable against malicious administrators, because again we have to assume that they know any pre-shared password. Furthermore a protocol based on pre-shared passwords is unfeasible for highly distributed use cases where new communication endpoints regularly join the network (requirement F4).

Vulnerable Against Relay Attacks. Protocols are vulnerable against insider attacks if they use long-term secrets to establish the secure channel. This attack can be avoided by conducting an ephemeral key exchange during the attestation process. Stumpf et al. [14] propose to link remote attestation with a Diffie-Hellman key exchange by including the ephemeral public keys in the quote.

---

[3] https://github.com/tpm2-software/tpm2-tss-engine.

After the attestation is complete, both endpoints derive a symmetric key from the established secret and use it to encrypt all subsequent communication. While this thwarts the insider attack and provides forward secrecy (S5 and F3), including ephemeral public keys in the quote can introduce vulnerabilities against relay attacks (c.f. [6,16]). During this attack the adversary relays messages to the original trusted system in order to answer another attestation challenge on his own. Protocols directly based on Stumpf's approach [1,8] are also susceptible to this attack and do not fulfill requirement S6.

Other Protocols. Gasmi et al. [6] and Armknecht et al. [2] embed the remote attestation process into a standard TLS handshake. While this fixes the vulnerability against relay attacks, there are drawbacks to this approach. Since attestation data is included in the TLS handshake, a modified TLS implementation has to be used. Tying remote attestation to the TLS library conflates protection goals and complicates code base updates (requirement F4). Furthermore, these protocols use the *Secret Key Attestation Evidence (SKAE)* feature of the TPM 1.2 specification, which is not included in recent versions anymore. In a similar fashion, Lan et al. [9] add direct anonymous attestation (DAA) to a TLS handshake. This approach also uses a modified TLS stack, does not support mutual attestation and requires fresh AIK re-enrollments for each handshake, which is very costly in distributed environments (requirements F1 and F4). Also neither of these proposals offer working code or usable libraries.

We provide a detailed comparison of the discussed protocols during the evaluation in Sect. 4 (c.f. Tables 2 and 3). All in all no existing protocol fulfills all requirements we have for a remote attestation protocol.

2.3   Attacks on IDSCP

The Industrial Data Space Communication Protocol (IDSCP) is a remote attestation protocol introduced by Lux and Brost in 2018 [10]. It relies on an underlying standard TLS connection to provide authentication and channel encryption. However, unlike with previous TLS-based proposals, the remote attestation is not directly included in the TLS handshake. Instead a mutual attestation is conducted as soon as the standard TLS connection has been established between both trusted endpoints. During this attestation phase both sides draw and exchange random nonces to protect against replay attacks. These nonces are then used to generate a TPM-signed quote containing a selection of the current PCR values on each trusted platform. Finally the quotes' PCR values and signatures are verified by each side, thereby mutually confirming the integrity of both trusted software stacks. In order to link the underlying TLS session with the conducted remote attestation, the quotes also contain a hash of the respective TLS certificates that authenticated the initial TLS handshake. By comparing this hash with his own TLS public key fingerprint, each verifier can check if the attested remote endpoint operates on the "right" TLS channel. A complete description of the IDSCP protocol is given in [10]. For convenience purposes we include an overview of the protocol handshake in the appendix (c.f. Table 4).

Instead of conducting a separate key agreement, IDSCP relies on the underlying TLS channel to encrypt transmitted data. Since no modified or enhanced TLS handshake is necessary, IDSCP can be easily implemented using any standard TLS library. This is a clear advantage over previous TLS-based remote attestation protocols such as [4] and [6]. However, conflating the security goals of the encryption layer and the attestation protocol introduces new vulnerabilities. The attestation part of IDSCP simply presupposes the security of the encrypted TLS channel without considering that the respective attacker models differ. As a result, the protocol becomes vulnerable against an insider attack similar to the previously mentioned one on Cheng's proposal [4], if the underlying TLS key establishment is performed by transmitting an encrypted pre-master secret. An insider attacker, who has access to the TLS private keys of the trusted platform, can intercept the pre-master secret and subsequently decrypt any communication that should be decipherable solely by the trusted software stack of the attested endpoint. Even though not explicitly mentioned by the IDSCP specification, this attack can be avoided by forcing both endpoints to agree on a TLS cipher suite that features perfect forward secrecy (PFS).

Scenario for a Relay Attack. However, even when IDSCP uses perfect forward secrecy, in certain situations the protocol is still vulnerable against a variant of the classical relay attack. During a relay attack the adversary typically conducts a legitimate remote attestation with the trusted platform and uses the response to forge attestation evidence for his own platform. While relay attacks on Stumpf's protocol are performed this way (c.f. [6,16]), the attack on IDSCP requires a modified approach. More concretely, we extend the classical relay attack by using a legitimate third-party application on the trusted platform that also offers an attestation endpoint. The key to this attack is that these two endpoints, while on the same platform, do not implement the same attestation protocol. Even though the security impact of multiple attestation endpoints is seldom being considered, this is a very realistic attack vector for IDSCP. Since the Industrial Data Space architecture supports distributed data processing across multiple companies [12], third-party applications are deployed on trusted platforms.

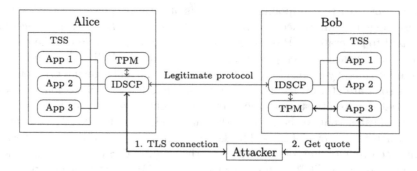

Fig. 1. Scenario for the relay attack on IDSCP.

As a result it is possible that – in addition to the general IDSCP endpoint – a second remote attestation endpoint is provided by one of the legitimate data processing applications. This scenario is depicted in Fig. 1. The communication is routed through the IDSCP endpoints on both Alice's and Bob's system. In order to intercept information intended for Bob's trusted software stack, the attacker first establishes a TLS connection with Alice's IDSCP endpoint. Then the attacker contacts the additional attestation endpoint in Bob's trusted software stack (in this case app 3) to retrieve the quoting information he needs to complete the IDSCP handshake. Note that app 3 is a legitimate data processing application and a valid part of Bob's trusted software stack (TSS), so the PCR fingerprints of the generated quote are as Alice expects them to be. Hence Alice will trust this IDSCP channel, even though it is controlled by the attacker.

Relay Attack on IDSCP. If the IDSCP protocol is executed properly, each trusted platform first performs a TLS handshake, chooses the Diffie-Hellman key pair and signs the public part with the TLS private key. In order to extract information intended only for a trusted platform, the attacker has to perform these steps on a different machine. Fig. 2 shows how an internal attacker can intercept encrypted information from an IDSCP channel. In this example Alice acts as honest verifier, who intends to establish an attested IDSCP connection to Bob's trusted platform. As before, we assume the strongest attacker to be an administrator attempting to intercept information that should be decipherable only by Bob's unmodified trusted software stack. This attacker has access to Bob's TLS long-term secrets and can use them to conduct his own TLS handshake with the remote verifier (Alice), thereby impersonating an endpoint on Bob's legitimate trusted system (1). The goal of the attack is to establish an attested connection with a computer system that is not the trusted platform it claims to be. Note that even though an insider attacker typically has access to Bob's legitimate trusted platform, he cannot use the original system to do this, because that would change the PCRs and hence reveal the attack.

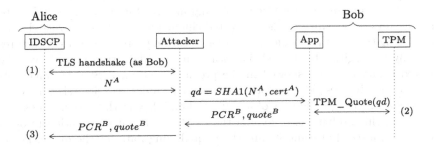

Fig. 2. Relay attack on the IDSCP protocol. Not all messages are shown.

After the TLS connection is established, the attacker needs to present a valid quote during the subsequent attestation phase of the IDSCP protocol. This quote needs to be signed by Bob's original TPM and has to contain both the correct nonce and the remote TLS certificate. Clearly such a quote can only be created by Bob's original trusted platform. In a classical relay attack the adversary would try to extract the quote by initiating another IDSCP handshake with Bob's trusted platform and relay Alice's nonce as his own. However, this approach does not work for IDSCP, because Alice expects the quote to contain both her nonce and her TLS certificate. According to the protocol specification, Bob's unmodified IDSCP endpoint only generates quotes containing TLS certificates that the remote party used for establishing the connection. Hence the attacker would need to sign a key exchange with Alice's TLS long-term secret, which he does not know. Instead he contacts the additional attestation endpoint in Bob's trusted software stack and requests a quote from there. To make the quote look as if generated by the IDSCP endpoint, the attacker calculates the hash of Alice's nonce and her TLS certificate – both values are known to him – and uses it as his own nonce (2). Assuming that the additional attestation endpoint processes the requested qualifying data unaltered, this generates a quote that convinces Alice (3). Since the hash value is indistinguishable from a random nonce, neither honest party can detect this interference. Once the handshake is completed, Alice is confident that she can securely send information to Bob's trusted platform, even though the attacker intercepts them on a different machine.

The IDSCP protocol is vulnerable because it includes public keys in the quote. Attestation protocols using only randomly drawn nonces as qualifying data, such as [2,6,9], are not vulnerable to this attack. However, these protocols have drawbacks that make them unsuitable for use cases such as the Industrial Data Space (c.f. Sect. 2.2). Hence there is still a need for a simple and easily usable remote attestation protocol that is not susceptible to this type of attack.

3   A Secure Protocol

A secure protocol needs to conduct a remote attestation and establish encrypted channels between the endpoints. On their own, both of these tasks have been solved. The problem we face when designing an attestation protocol is how to bind the keys responsible for the encrypted channel to the attested trusted platform. Doing this right is vital for a secure attestation protocol, because it ensures that only the legitimate trusted platform can read data transmitted over the attested channel. As we showed in the previous section, IDSCP is vulnerable to active man-in-the-middle attacks because it includes security relevant information such as the public part of a Diffie-Hellman key in the quote. A possible solution to this problem is to extend the PCRs with that information prior to attestation, instead of using it directly as qualifying data for the quote. Doing so shows a verifier that the Diffie-Hellman key pair used for key establishment was in fact generated on the trusted platform itself, while avoiding the vulnerability against relay attacks. However, this solution is not feasible in practice. Since each established channel requires a new key exchange, the legitimate PCR values will change constantly. As a result the measurement logs that verifiers have to check become large and extremely cluttered. This makes it very difficult to update and maintain a trusted software stack in a dynamic and distributed environment. Another approach for binding the ephemeral public keys to the trusted platform is to sign them with the attestation identity key (AIK). Since only the TPM can sign with the AIK, this proves that the key originates from the trusted platform. Also it prevents relay attacks, since the key exchange is completely independent of the quote. However, the AIK is a restricted key and cannot be used for signing external data. It can only sign data structures that have been created by the TPM, such as quotes. This property of the AIK is in fact very important for the remote attestation, since otherwise the platform could use the TPM to certify a fake quote (e.g. with wrong PCRs). While this makes an AIK-certified key exchange impossible with the now outdated TPM version 1.2, there are more options available with a recent TPM in version 2.0. By implementing a TPM-managed key exchange, we can sign ephemeral keys with the AIK, thereby binding the key establishment to the trusted platform.

3.1   Protocol Design

A secure remote attestation protocol has to protect against internal attackers with access to platform secrets. However, TLS by design does not consider this type of adversary. As previously shown, combining the TLS-based encryption with attestation conflates security goals and complicates protocol applications. To avoid this we choose not to use TLS as underlying protocol. Instead we concentrate on establishing a shared secret that is guaranteed to be available only to the attested platform. This secret can then be used for manual encryption or as a key for an independent TLS layer. We assume that prior to the start of the protocol both participants have taken ownership of their TPM and created a storage root key. Furthermore they should have performed the AIK enrollment process and have their AIK certificates signed by a privacy CA. Our attestation protocol consists of three phases, which are shown in Table 1. The semantic of the functions as well as the parameter names follow the TPM 2.0 specification.

Initiation. During the *initiation phase*, both endpoints first create a TPM key template for appropriate encryption keys, which will be used in a later phase. Then random nonces are created and exchanged (steps 1 and 2). While the size of the nonces is not specified, it is recommended to use at least 160 bits of random data to ensure proper quote freshness. Furthermore, both sides transmit a selection of PCR numbers that they expect to be included in the quote.

Attestation. Afterwards the *attestation phase* is responsible for exchanging and verifying quotes. This is done in accordance with the TCG trusted attestation protocol [15]. For the sake of simplicity Table 1 only shows the explicit attestation. Nevertheless the other specified attestation types may be used as well. Since this affects only the TPM function calls and the contents of the quote, but

Table 1. Our proposed attestation protocol

	Initiation phase
A, B	: $dhTemplate \leftarrow$ TPMT_PUBLIC(decrypt, KEY_SCHEME_ECDH)
A	: Create a non-predictable nonce N^A
$A \rightarrow B$:	$N^A, PCRSel^A$ ... (1)
B	: Create a non-predictable nonce N^B
$A \leftarrow B$:	$N^B, PCRSel^B$ ... (2)
	Attestation phase
A	: $(quoted^A, quoteSig^A) \leftarrow$ TPM2_Quote($akHandle^A, N^B, PCRSel^B$)
$A \rightarrow B$:	$PCR^A, (quoted^A, quoteSig^A), akCert^A$ ... (3)
B	: Verify CA signature of $akCert^A$
B	: Verify $quoteSig^A$ is a valid signature of $quoted^A$ under $akCert^A$
B	: Verify $quoted^A$ contains expected PCR^A and N^B
B	: $(quoted^B, quoteSig^B) \leftarrow$ TPM2_Quote($akHandle^B, N^A, PCRSel^A$)
$A \leftarrow B$:	$PCR^B, (quoted^B, quoteSig^B), akCert^B$ ... (4)
A	: Verify CA signature of $akCert^B$
A	: Verify $quoteSig^B$ is a valid signature of $quoted^B$ under $akCert^B$
A	: Verify $quoted^B$ contains expected PCR^B and N^A
	Key establishment phase
A	: $dh^A \leftarrow$ TPM2_Create($srkHandle^A, dhTemplate$)
A	: $dhHandle^A \leftarrow$ TPM2_Load($srkHandle^A, dh^A.private, dh^A.public$)
A	: $(dhCertInfo^A, dhSig^A) \leftarrow$ TPM2_Certify($dhHandle^A, akHandle^A, N^B$)
$A \rightarrow B$:	$dh^A.public, (dhCertInfo^A, dhSig^A)$ ... (5)
B	: Verify $dhSig^A$ is a valid signature of $dhCertInfo^A$ under $akCert^A$
B	: Verify $dhCertInfo^A$ contains expected $dh^A.public$ and N^B
B	: $dh^B \leftarrow$ TPM2_Create($srkHandle^B, dhTemplate$)
B	: $dhHandle^B \leftarrow$ TPM2_Load($srkHandle^B, dh^B.private, dh^B.public$)
B	: $(dhCertInfo^B, dhSig^B) \leftarrow$ TPM2_Certify($dhHandle^B, akHandle^B, N^A$)
B	: $Z \leftarrow$ TPM2_ECDH_ZGen($dhHandle^B, dh^A.public$)
$A \leftarrow B$:	$dh^B.public, (dhCertInfo^B, dhSig^B)$ ... (6)
A	: Verify $dhSig^B$ is a valid signature of $dhCertInfo^B$ under $akCert^B$
A	: Verify $dhCertInfo^B$ contains expected $dh^B.public$ and N^A
A	: $Z \leftarrow$ TPM2_ECDH_ZGen($dhHandle^A, dh^B.public$)
$A \leftrightarrow B$:	Encrypt messages using secret $k := KDF(Z)$

not the transmitted messages, our protocol is agnostic about the concrete attestation type. With explicit attestation, both participants execute TPM2_Quote in order to create a quote that is signed by the TPM with the attestation identity key. Only the previously received nonce is included as qualifying data. Afterwards the quote, its signature, the values of the requested PCRs and the AIK certificate are transmitted to the verifier (steps 3 and 4). Once the attestation information has been passed to the remote side, the AIK certificate, quote signature and quote information are being verified in that order. Since the protocol supports mutual attestation, both parties have to perform these protocol steps.

If any of the verification steps fail, either of the endpoints terminates the protocol handshake. After the attestation phase has been completed successfully, both endpoints have verified the integrity of the other trusted platform.

Key Establishment. Finally the *key establishment phase* establishes a shared secret between the two endpoints that is bound to the attested trusted platforms. For this we conduct a TPM-managed Elliptic Curve Diffie-Hellman (ECDH) key exchange. The TPM 2.0 specification conveniently offers functions for one-pass and two-pass key exchange protocols. Since we only want to conduct an ephemeral key exchange, the one-pass version is sufficient. Usually the one-pass key exchange is conducted asymmetrically using TPM2_ECDH_KeyGen. However, this is not feasible for our protocol, because we need to sign both ephemeral public keys with the restricted AIK. Because the TPM2_ECDH_KeyGen function directly outputs the generated ephemeral public point without proof of TPM ownership, we cannot use the AIK to sign this key. Also, in order to keep the protocol implementation as simple as possible, it is beneficial to perform a symmetric key establishment where both sides execute the same steps.

To solve these problems we conduct the key exchange by creating both ephemeral keys with TPM2_Create and invoking the TPM2_ECDH_ZGen function twice (c.f. Table 1). At first Alice creates a new ephemeral ECDH key pair by invoking the TPM2_Create method with the ECDH key template created earlier. It is important that this key is generated as a wrapped sub key instead of a root key using TPM2_Create_Primary. This is because primary keys are derived from the seldom changing platform secrets, while the ephemeral keys need to be randomly drawn for each handshake. After the ephemeral key pair has been created, it needs to be loaded into the TPM using TPM2_Load. Since the key pair has been generated in the TPM instead of the CPU, its public part can then be signed by the AIK using the TPM2_Certify function It is important to include the previously exchanged nonces into this signature, because otherwise the key exchange may be vulnerable to replay attacks. Finally Alice sends the public part of the ephemeral key, as well as the certification information and the signature to Bob (step 5). Bob can check if the received ephemeral key was in fact generated by the trusted system by verifying the signature with Alice's AIK certificate. He also checks if his nonce is included in the certification information. Then Bob uses TPM2_Create and TPM2_Certify to generate his own ephemeral ECDH key and AIK signature in the same way. By invoking TPM2_ECDH_ZGen with a handle on his own ECDH key and Alice's public key, Bob uses his TPM to calculate the shared secret Z. Finally he transmits his ephemeral public key and the corresponding signature back to Alice (step 6). After receiving Bob's public key and signature, Alice performs the same steps to verify the key and calculate the shared secret on her end. If any of the verification steps fail, either of the endpoints terminates the protocol handshake. Otherwise the protocol handshake completes with the establishment of the shared secret. Usually a symmetric encryption key is derived from the shared secret via a key derivation function (KDF), which protects the established channel. The nature of the KDF and the subsequent encryption is not specified in the protocol handshake. We furthermore do not have any specific requirements for the network protocol that is used to send and receive the messages shown in Table 1.

3.2 Protocol Implementation

A reference implementation of our protocol is available (see footnote 2). To access TPM 2.0 devices we use Microsoft's TPM Software Stack. Since this software stack interfaces both physical TPM devices and a TPM 2.0 simulator, it is suitable for development purposes as well as productive use. As there are bindings for other programming languages, the protocol can be adopted easily for other platforms. We create the ephemeral ECDH keys using the NIST P-256 elliptic curve and SHA-256 message digests. The attestation handshake and all subsequent communication is conducted over the standard WebSocket protocol. After a successful handshake the symmetric channel encryption is achieved using the Java Crypto API and an AES-256 encryption with PKCS#7 padding.

4 Evaluation

In this section we analyze the presented protocol in terms of the previously defined security and functional requirements. We also compare our approach to previously proposed attestation protocols. Finally show how we verify our protocol using the Tamarin protocol verifier.

4.1 Security Analysis

In Sect. 2.1 we defined seven security goals S1 to S7. Now we show that our proposal fulfills all of these requirements. The security goals of authentication (S1) and platform integrity verification (S2) are satisfied by the attestation phase of the protocol. This phase performs a standard remote attestation of both endpoints by exchanging quotes that are signed with the platforms' attestation identity keys (AIK). Even an insider attacker with access to long-term secrets cannot forge an AIK signature, because the private key is only accessible to the TPM. Hence the AIK signature ensures that the verifier actually communicates with the correct platform, which fulfills the authentication requirement (S1). Naturally the exchanged quotes also attest to the integrity of the trusted platforms (S2), because they contain the requested selection of PCR values for the verifiers to check. Furthermore our protocol offers a secure key establishment (S3) by performing a Diffie-Hellman key exchange in the final phase of the handshake. Unlike with the proposal of Stumpf [14] and its variants, our key establishment is authenticated by the AIK. This enables the verifier to check that the ephemeral keys have in fact been generated on the authenticated trusted platform in the already attested state. As a result, our protocol is not vulnerable against the attacks defined by S4 to S7. The nonces that are exchanged during the initiation phase protect against replay attacks (S4). The protocol is also not vulnerable against insider attacks (S5), because nothing is signed or encrypted with a non-TPM key that an insider attacker could use to his advantage. Especially the ephemeral keys are not signed with external long-term secrets, but are instead authenticated by the AIK, which is not available to the insider attacker. The main advantage of our protocol over IDSCP is its resilience against relay attacks even with a second attestation endpoint (S6 and S7). The key difference is that our protocol uses only nonces as qualifying data for the quote, not the hash of other security critical information. This prevents the presented relay attack with an additional attestation endpoint. A further advantage of our protocol is that the private ephemeral keys are generated by the TPM and never leave it. Therefore our protocol is not vulnerable against side-channel attacks on the CPU. Protocols that generate the ephemeral keys on the processor need to trust that they are not being disclosed, which is a severe disadvantage over creating them in the TPM. Table 2 compares the security properties of our protocol with previous proposals discussed in Sect. 2.2. For better comparison of vulnerable protocols, the second column shows the weakest attacker that successfully breaks one of the security requirements. We distinguish between an insider attacker (I), who knows non-TPM secrets, and an external adversary (E). Also the adversary can either be passive (P) or an active Dolev-Yao attacker (A). This notation gives an active insider attacker (IA) as strongest adversary, while a passive external attacker (EP) is the weakest adversary. The checkmark after the attacker properties shows if the attack is transparent (✓) or detectable by one of the protocol participants (✗). In summary, our protocol as well as the proposals of Armknecht and Lan are secure against all presented attacks. However, as already discussed in Sect. 2.2, in practice the latter protocols have disadvantages both in terms of security and functionality.

Table 2. Comparison of security properties.

Proposal	Attacker	S1	S2	S3	S4	S5	S6	S7	Remarks
Sailer [13]	EA (✗)	✗	✓	–	✓	–	–	–	No key exchange
Coker [5]	–	✓	✓	–	✓	–	–	–	No key exchange
Goldman [7]	IP (✓)	✓	✓	✗	✓	✗	✗	✗	PFS not mentioned
Cheng [4]	IP (✓)	✓	✓	✗	✓	✗	✗	✗	
IDSCP	IP (✓)	✓	✓	✗	✓	✗	✗	✗	
Aziz [3]	IA (✗)	✓	✓	✗	✓	✗	✗	✗	PFS not mentioned
Stumpf [14]	EA (✓)	✓	✓	✗	✓	✓	✗	✗	
IDSCP (PFS)	IA (✗)	✓	✓	✗	✓	✓	✓	✗	
Zhou [16]	IA (✗)	✓	✓	✗	✓	✗	✓	✗	
Armknecht [2]	–	✓	✓	✓	✓	✓	✓	✓	Only TPM 1.2
Lan [9]	–	✓	✓	✓	✓	✓	✓	✓	
Our protocol	–	✓	✓	✓	✓	✓	✓	✓	**Only TPM 2.0**

4.2   Protocol Properties

Considering the functional requirements, our protocol clearly supports mutual attestation (F1). Since the protocol explicitly separates attestation from key establishment, re-attestation is possible without a key change (F2). Finally, conducting a new ephemeral key exchange for each protocol handshake gives the forward secrecy property (F3). In terms of overhead our approach is of a similar complexity as IDSCP (F4). Our reference implementation has about 1700 lines of code, while IDSCP has about 2000. Furthermore, we have no link with a TLS protocol instance and are independent of the network stack. On the other hand, since our protocol calculates the key exchange directly on the TPM hardware instead of the much faster CPU, a performance impact is to be expected. Table 3 compares the functional properties of our protocol to the previous proposals.

Table 3. Comparison of functional properties.

Proposal	F1	F2	F3	F4	Remarks
Sailer [13]	✗	–	✗	Low	
Coker [5]	✗	–	✗	Medium	
Goldman [7]	✗	✓	(✓)	High	
Cheng [4]	✗	–	✗	Low	
IDSCP	✓	✗	✗	Low	
Aziz [3]	✓	✗	(✓)	Medium	
Stumpf [14]	✗	✗	✓	Low	
IDSCP (PFS)	✓	✗	✓	Low	
Zhou [16]	✓	✗	✓	Medium	
Armknecht [2]	✓	✓	✓	High	Only TPM 1.2
Lan [9]	✗	✗	✓	High	
Our protocol	✓	✓	✓	**Medium**	**Only TPM 2.0**

4.3   Formal Verification

In addition to the informal security analysis, we also verified our protocol using the Tamarin prover [11]. Our main goal in doing so is to show that – unlike IDSCP – our protocol is secure even with an additional attestation endpoint (security goal S7). First we modeled both our protocol and IDSCP with Tamarin's Diffie-Hellman equational theory. Then we defined the security requirements as Tamarin trace properties quantifying over the attacker's knowledge. These trace properties determine that for a secure protocol the attacker must not learn the established shared secret. We also added an additional rule that allows the attacker to retrieve signed quotes with any qualifying data.

This models the additional attestation endpoint on the trusted platform. If the rule is active, Tamarin in fact finds the man-in-the-middle attack on IDSCP we presented in Sect. 2.3. In contrast, Tamarin correctly verifies all security properties on our protocol, even with the additional attestation endpoint available to the attacker. All theorem definitions of both IDSCP and our protocol are available for verification (see footnote 2).

5   Conclusion

In this work we evaluated existing attestation protocols in terms of security and functionality. We found that many existing protocols are either vulnerable against insider or relay attacks, or depend on outdated TPM specifications. Furthermore we showed that an actively used remote attestation protocol (IDSCP) is vulnerable against a variant of relay attacks that assumes the existence of additional attestation endpoints. In response to this threat we proposed and analyzed a lightweight remote attestation protocol that is not vulnerable against this type of attack. Our protocol is based on the TPM 2.0 specification and offers mutual attestation, re-attestation and shared key establishment with perfect forward secrecy. Unlike previous proposals, our protocol generates secret keys exclusively inside the TPM, which protects against side-channel attacks on the CPU. Keeping our protocol completely independent of the underlying network stack makes it very flexible and easy to adapt for any use case specific requirements. Finally we analyzed the security of our protocol both informally as well as by modeling its security properties with the Tamarin theorem prover. A ready-to-use protocol implementation is publicly available as well (see footnote 2).

As future work we plan to implement our protocol for other platforms and more TPM software stacks. We also intend to evaluate the performance of our protocol more rigorously in the Industrial Data Space as an actual productive use case. Furthermore our protocol can be extended to also support direct anonymous attestation (DAA).

A   The Industrial Data Space Communication Protocol

Table 4 illustrates the messages sent during an IDSCP handshake. A complete description of the IDSCP protocol is given in [10]. The reference implementation of IDSCP is available on Github (see footnote 1).

Table 4. IDSCP remote attestation protocol

TLS handshake
$A \leftrightarrow B$: Establish a TLS channel with certificates $cert^A$ and $cert^B$

Initiation phase	
$A \rightarrow B$: Non-predictable nonce N^A	(1)
$A \leftarrow B$: Non-predictable nonce N^B	(2)

Attestation phase	
A $\quad$: $(quoted^A, quoteSig^A) \leftarrow$ TPM_Quote$(akHandle^A, SHA1(N^B, cert^B))$	
$A \rightarrow B$: $PCR^A, (quoted^A, quoteSig^A), akCert^A$	(3)
B : $(quoted^B, quoteSig^B) \leftarrow$ TPM_Quote$(akHandle^B, SHA1(N^A, cert^A))$	
$A \leftarrow B$: $PCR^B, (quoted^B, quoteSig^B), akCert^B$	(4)

Verification phase
A $\quad$: Verify CA signature of $akCert^B$
A $\quad$: Verify $quoteSig^B$ is a valid signature of $quoted^B$ under $akCert^B$
A $\quad$: Verify $quoted^B$ contains expected PCR^B and $SHA1(N^A, cert^A)$
B : Verify CA signature of $akCert^A$
B : Verify $quoteSig^A$ is a valid signature of $quoted^A$ under $akCert^A$
B : Verify $quoted^A$ contains expected PCR^A and $SHA1(N^B, cert^B)$

References

1. Akram, R.N., Markantonakis, K., Mayes, K., Bonnefoi, P.F., Sauveron, D., Chaumette, S.: An efficient, secure and trusted channel protocol for avionics wireless networks. In: 35th Digital Avionics Systems Conference, pp. 1–10. IEEE (2016)
2. Armknecht, F., et al.: An efficient implementation of trusted channels based on OpenSSL. In: 3rd ACM Workshop on Scalable Trusted Computing, pp. 41–50 (2008)
3. Aziz, N., Udzir, N., Mahmod, R.: Extending TLS with mutual attestation for platform integrity assurance. J. Commun. **9**(1), 63–72 (2014)
4. Cheng, S., Bing, L., Yang, X., Yixian, Y., Li, Z., Han, Y.: A security-enhanced remote platform integrity attestation scheme. In: 5th Conference on Wireless Communications, Networking and Mobile Computing, pp. 1–4. IEEE (2009)
5. Coker, G., et al.: Principles of remote attestation. Int. J. Inf. Secur. **10**(2), 63–81 (2011). https://doi.org/10.1007/s10207-011-0124-7
6. Gasmi, Y., Sadeghi, A.R., Stewin, P., Unger, M., Asokan, N.: Beyond secure channels. In: 2007 ACM workshop on Scalable trusted computing, pp. 30–40 (2007)
7. Goldman, K., Perez, R., Sailer, R.: Linking remote attestation to secure tunnel endpoints. In: 1st ACM workshop on Scalable trusted computing, pp. 21–24 (2006)
8. Greveler, U., Justus, B., Löhr, D.: Mutual remote attestation: enabling system cloning for TPM based platforms. In: Meadows, C., Fernandez-Gago, C. (eds.) STM 2011. LNCS, vol. 7170, pp. 193–206. Springer, Heidelberg (2012). https://doi.org/10.1007/978-3-642-29963-6_14
9. Lan, A., Han, Z., Zhang, D., Jiang, Y., Liu, T., Li, M.: An anonymous remote attestation protocol to prevent masquerading attack. In: 11th International Conference on Autonomic and Trusted Computing, pp. 590–595. IEEE (2014)

10. Lux, M., Brost, G.: The industrial dataspace communication protocol. A protocol for remote attestation and secure data exchange (2018)
11. Meier, S., Schmidt, B., Cremers, C., Basin, D.: The TAMARIN prover for the symbolic analysis of security protocols. In: Sharygina, N., Veith, H. (eds.) CAV 2013. LNCS, vol. 8044, pp. 696–701. Springer, Heidelberg (2013). https://doi.org/10.1007/978-3-642-39799-8_48
12. Otto, B., Lohmann, S., Steinbuß, S., Teuscher, A.: IDS reference architecture model. Technical report, International Data Spaces Association (2018)
13. Sailer, R., Zhang, X., Jaeger, T., Van Doorn, L.: Design and implementation of a TCG-based integrity measurement architecture. In: USENIX Security symposium, vol. 13, pp. 223–238 (2004)
14. Stumpf, F., Tafreschi, O., Röder, P., Eckert, C., et al.: A robust integrity reporting protocol for remote attestation. In: Proceedings of the Workshop on Advances in Trusted Computing (WATC), p. 65. Citeseer (2006)
15. TCG: Trusted attestation protocol (TAP) information model. Technical report (2019)
16. Zhou, L., Zhang, Z.: Trusted channels with password-based authentication and TPM-based attestation. In: 2010 International Conference on Communications and Mobile Computing, vol. 1, pp. 223–227. IEEE (2010)

Security Processes

Improved Feature Engineering for Free-Text Keystroke Dynamics

Eden Abadi and Itay Hazan[(⊠)] [iD]

IBM Cybersecurity Center of Excellence, Beer Sheva, Israel
edena@ibm.com, itayha@il.ibm.com

Abstract. Free-text keystroke dynamics is a method of verifying users' identity based on their unique pattern of typing a spontaneous text on a keyboard. When applied in remote systems, it can add an additional layer of security that can detect compromised accounts. Therefore, service providers can be more certain that remote systems accounts would not be compromised by malicious attackers. Free-text keystroke dynamics usually involve the extraction of n-graphs, which represent the latency between *n* consecutive events. These n-graphs are then integrated with one of the various existing machine learning algorithms. To the best of our knowledge, n-graphs are the most widely used feature engineering for free text keystroke dynamics. We present *extended-n-graphs,* an improved version of the commonly used n-graphs, based on several extended metrics that outperform the traditionally used basic n-graphs. Our technique was evaluated on top of the gradient boosting algorithm, best performing algorithm on basic n-graphs and several additional algorithms such as random forest, K-NN, SVM and MLP. Our empirical results show encouraging 4% improvement in the Area Under the Curve (AUC) when evaluated on a publicly used benchmark.

Keywords: Keystroke dynamics · Free text · Feature engineering

1 Introduction

Remotely accessing sensitive systems such as governmental, financial, and healthcare systems via the Internet has become a normal routine in our everyday life. Through these systems, service providers give users the ability to view sensitive information and easily perform actions when at home or in remote locations. However, the ever-growing dependence on these systems to store valuable information and perform actions has made users increasingly vulnerable to attacks. But, while technology advances rapidly, so do the hazardous in it. Ultimately, today's online hackers pose threats not only to individuals, but also to large companies and governments that due to the recent worldwide pandemic events increased the number of employees that are working from home.

Password is still one of the most used authentication methods to detect attacks and prevent unauthorized access. Nevertheless, this method has weak spots that attackers can use to gain unauthorized access and perform actions on other users' behalf. One such weak spot is that they only verify the user in the beginning of the session. If attackers managed to hijack the authenticated session, they can remotely control the

© Springer Nature Switzerland AG 2020
K. Markantonakis and M. Petrocchi (Eds.): STM 2020, LNCS 12386, pp. 93–105, 2020.
https://doi.org/10.1007/978-3-030-59817-4_6

entire account. Another weak spot is that if attackers somehow managed to steal the password without the user knowing, they can access the user account and even lock him out. Stealing users' credentials can be done using various techniques such as shoulder surfing, keyloggers, brute force engines, etc. In another scenario the user can cooperate with the attackers to fool the service provider for example in online exams, that became more popular during the worldwide pandemic events that forced people to stay home. In that case the user shares unrightfully his credentials with the attackers so they will perform his tasks instead of him. One way to avoid that is using continuous authentication to continuously verify the user's identity and prevent such attacks during the session.

Keystroke dynamics (KD), which relies on the user's specific keyboard typing patterns, is one of the most emerging mechanisms for continuous authentication. Similar to handwriting and walking, keyboard typing often contains unique user behavior patterns. The main advantages of this method are that it is cost-effective, seamless, and is relatively easy to implement [11].

KD techniques are usually divided to two different approaches: (i) Fixed-text, which refers to verifying the users' identity by short and structured texts (e.g., username and password), and (ii) Free-text, which refers to verifying the users identity based on unstructured and spontaneous texts (e.g., email messages). Fixed text KD is often applied to the username and password that are typed during the initial authentication phase. In this case, the typing rhythm is checked alongside the correctness of the username and password. However, this does not prevent attacks later throughout the session and is usually not referred to as continuous authentication. Free-text KD, on the other hand, can prevent attacks throughout a user's session, as long as he/she keep typing text. This method is generally carried out by analyzing the individual's unique typing rhythm when the text is longer, unseen previously and does not necessarily entered only at the beginning of the session. Therefore, due to its ability to verify the users throughout the session, it is usually referred as continuous authentication and it is the main focus of our research.

As in many other machine-learning-based solutions, free-text KD solutions are assembled from a learning algorithm and feature engineering phase. The most well-known and used features for free-text KD are *n-graphs* on top of the extracted *n-grams*. An n-gram is a text substring of size *n*. An n-graph is usually considered the latency between the first and the last event of a certain n-gram with *n* events (which is not necessarily the same *n* as the n-gram's). Among n-graphs are di-graph and tri-graphs, which are private cases of it. Di-graphs use the latency of exactly two consecutive events and tri-graphs use the latency of exactly three consecutive events. To the best of our knowledge, di-graphs, on all of its forms (i.e. press-to-release, press-to-press, release-to-release, release-to-press) are the most widely used feature extraction in free-text KD [1–6].

The main problem with n-graphs is that their implementation can cause the data to not be represented correctly according to the natural distribution of it. This problem occurs when an n-gram recurs several times within a segment of the data which, causes a list of latencies for one n-graph feature instead of just one latency. As previously seen, in such cases researchers tend to take the mean [3, 16]. However, by doing so they implicitly assume that the data has a certain distribution which is not necessarily true. Another option is taking the first or the last latency; but doing so eliminates some of the information as well. Another problem with n-graphs, as shown by Sim et al. [17] is that when used in different contexts, i.e. longer n-grams, the importance/impact of the n-graph to the algorithms decision can vary. For example the di-gram 'in' as a word or as part of the word 'thing' will have different importance. For that reason Sim et al. suggested to use di-graphs in the context of words (which are basically longer or same size n-grams) as part of the feature space.

To solve the first problem we suggest the use of several different metrics instead of just mean. In addition, to extend the solution given by Sim et al. to the second problem, we suggest to derive much more features from each n-gram and not just the end-to-end latency or the di-graphs within the n-gram.

This work focuses on a novel feature extraction method for free-text KD. Our method consists of four steps: finding common n-grams for each user; splitting text into different windows (i.e. segments), where each window is evaluated independently; collecting relevant data for each n-gram; and calculating an extended feature set for each n-gram, which consists of its recurring list of n-graphs. We refer to this feature extraction method as *extended n-graphs*.

We evaluated our method, using set of different algorithms such as gradient boosting, random forest, K-NN, SVM and MLP, which were previously used in the field of keystroke dynamics (elaborated in Sect. 2) and applied them on the Perez keystroke dataset [15]. Our focus was on the best performing algorithm among them, which was gradient boosting, in which we demonstrate a 4% improvement using the extended n-graphs method on top of the basic existing n-graphs method with mean combination of recurring n-grams.

The structure of our paper is as follows. Section 2 depicts the related work in continuous authentication using free-text analysis. Section 3 presents the tested dataset. Section 4 elaborates on our method's feature extraction process. Section 5 includes the findings of our experiments with a comparison to different methods and Sect. 6 concludes the research.

2   Related Work

Research on keystroke dynamics started back in 1980 when Gaines et al. [6] investigated the relationship between user typing rhythms and identity. They found that it is possible to distinguish between users by using only several selected di-graphs. Later, in 1995, Shepherd et al. [1] showed even better results when measuring only latencies between keystrokes and durations of keystrokes and calculating the averages and variances globally. Their study tested only four different individuals, where even this very simple feature engineering was a good start in identifying the users.

Dowland et al. [2] attempted to use a more complex feature set including di-graphs, tri-graphs, and word latency as features, together with a distance-based classifier for classification. The authors achieved a False Acceptance Rate (FAR) of 4.9% with a 0% False Rejection Rate (FRR) over 35 users. More research on the subject was done by Gunetti et al. [3, 4]. They used free-text keystroke dynamics for authentication with di-graph latency with what they refer as disorder of the features and a distance-based classifier. Disorder is defined as the sum of differences between two arrays of the same length, or in other words the L1 loss between them. Eventually, they attained a FAR of 3.16% for an FRR of 0.02% for a full session prediction on 40 legitimate users and 62 impostors.

Messerman et al. [5] presented a non-intrusive verification scheme that continuously verifies the user identity using free-text KD. Their solution is an extension of the results presented by Gunetti et al. [3, 4]. They used n-graphs and a distance-based classifier that achieved an internal FAR of 2.02% and an external FAR of 2.61%, while the FRR was 1.84%. Similarly, Alsultan et al. [7] used timing features with Euclidian distance to find the level of similarity. Their main purpose was to reduce the number of training samples required by the system to identify the user therefore they use a unique key-pairs approach based on their keyboard adjacency dividing them into five groups. Eventually they achieved a FAR of 21% and an FRR of 17% but with a much lower number of training samples compared to others.

Ahmed et al. [8] evaluated deep learning architecture instead of classical machine learning algorithms. In their paper, they presented an analysis of keystrokes di-graphs and used a neural network to predict missing di-graphs based on the relation of the monitored keys. Their experiment, which consisted of 53 participants in a heterogeneous environment, yielded an FRR of 4.82% with FAR of 0.015%,

Kang et al. [9] evaluated the connection between the type of keyboard and the effectiveness of free-text user authentication. The authors used several well-known classification algorithms such as K-NN, Parzen, and SVDD. They found that the best results for free-text keystroke authentication were achieved with a standard PC keyboard, followed by a soft keyboard, and lastly a touch keyboard. The lowest equal error rate (EER) of 5%, which is FAR = FRR, was achieved by the PC keyboard with a long training set and test set (1000 characters). Their feature extraction was based on group division of the keyboard and calculating the press-to-release and release-to-press time between keyboard events.

Blomqvist [15] used gradient boosting, specifically XGBoost implementation [14] for keystroke dynamics. The author extracted a subset of the di-graphs: dwell time and flight time and managed to show an EER of 11.5% at the best case after tuning the algorithm. The author showed the results for fixed text keystroke dynamics, however we figured out that this algorithm could work well with free text keystroke dynamics as well.

Mondal et al. [13] introduced two new schemes to classify multiple users using continuous authentication. Their first scheme, which presented better or similar performance in most of the cases, called "pairwise user coupling" and is based on the idea of a tournament. The tournament is organized as a binary tree such that at the lower layer, each node contains exactly two random users. Using a trained model, the algorithm decides which user is more likely to be the test instance. The user with the higher likelihood moves to the upper layer. At each layer exactly half of the users are eliminated, and eventually the user who "won" the tournament is identified as the test instance. The extracted features are press-to-release and press-to-press. As for the classifiers, they created a multi-classifier fusion technique that includes the scores from an artificial neural network, decision tree, and SVM classifier. The best results achieved had an Accuracy of 89.7%.

Pin et al. [11] published in 2013 a survey of methods for keystroke dynamics. In this survey the authors presented a review of the many existing algorithms in field. They showed that the algorithms vary from basic machine learning algorithms such as SVM, K-NN, random forest, and neural network-based algorithms like back propagation such as MLP and Fast ANN and also discussed different research opportunities in the field. Ali et al. [10] published in 2015 a similar survey for keystroke dynamics on an updated list of methods, particularly more neural network-based algorithms and also discussed limitations and recommendations in the field. We refer the readers that would like to deepen in the different methods and their compartments to those two surveys. Both surveys summarized the results over different features and models since 1980 on both free-text and fixed-text keystroke dynamics.

In most of the literature addressing free-text keystroke dynamics, feature engineering is in the form of di-graph, tri-graph, or other types of n-graphs. In our method we chose to extend this feature engineering using several different methods of calculation and aggregation flow. We used several of the algorithms presented in this section to evaluate our method.

3 Suggested Method

To present our method, let us formally define the n-graphs on which our method is based on and extends. An n-graph is the delta time (i.e. latency) of an n-gram first and last events of presses and releases sequence. For example, below there is a sequence of two events, marking $\downarrow$ as press and $\uparrow$ as release: ($\downarrow$, 't', 623450), ($\uparrow$, 't', 623548). This sequence of events generates the n-gram 't' from which we obtain the feature p2r (i.e. press-to-release) with the delta time 98 ms: {p2r, "t": 98}. In our new method of feature extraction, that we refer to as extended-n-graphs, instead of extracting the same features for each specific n-graph, we calculate extended list of features on each one of the n-grams.

3.1 Extended n-graphs Overview

Usually in continuous authentication methods, one must first determine a segmentation method on the raw data such that the feature extraction and evaluation is done on each segment. Each segment would then be associated with exactly one feature vector, and when testing, the final score will be an aggregation of all the segmentations. In free-text keystroke dynamics it is common to use a fixed-size sliding windows with an overlapping window interval, such that each window is a segment. In our method we tried different window sizes and when tested, we used the mean to aggregate the windows scores.

After the division to segments, we move to extraction of a feature vector for each segment. The extraction has three main steps: First, for each common n-gram in the segment, we aggregate all its n-graph occurrences to a delta time list; Second, for each aggregated n-graph delta time list we apply the seven list extraction methods we defined (explained next), and extract list of values generated by this method. Third, for each list of values we calculate statistical features to describe their distribution (e.g. mean). Each of these statistical features will be a feature in our final feature vector.

3.2   Extracting List of Methods and Statistical Features

In the second step, we use a list of methods for every given n-gram inside the current window. This step is composed of the following methods on the lists of aggregated delta time lists:

- End-to-end delta time (E2E): calculates the list of delta time between the first press and the last release, in the entire n-gram.
- Each char press-to-release (EC): calculates for each char press-to-release delta times with respect to their location in the n-gram. For example, if we consider the n-gram 'meet', for each occurrence of this n-gram, the second letter - 'e' and the third letter 'e' will be calculated separately due to the fact they possess different location in the n-gram.
- Regular delta time (RDT): calculates for each consecutive *pair* of chars in the n-gram the press-to-release delta time with respect to their location in the n-gram.
- All combinations (AC): calculates all possible combinations of both press-to-release and release-to-press time (one list for all values) in the n-gram.
- All char delta time (ACDT): calculates a list of all chars delta times. As opposed to the AC, this one extracts the delta time for each individual key. Unlike the EC method, if we observe the previous example of the n-gram 'meet', in the ACDT method the second and the third occurrence of the letter 'e' will be calculated together regardless of their location in the n-gram.
- First delta time (FDT): calculates the list of first press-to-release or first release-to-press in the n-gram.
- Last delta time (LDT): calculates the list of last press-to-release or release-to-press in the n-gram.

We then calculate the following statistical features for every list of values: mean, standard deviation, minimum and maximum values. Thus, for each of those methods (for a given n-gram), we obtain four features describing their distribution.

3.3   Most Common n-grams

To somewhat reduce the number of sparse features and the very high dimensionality in the data, that happened due to short text on many different calculated n-grams, we focus only on a set of the most common n-grams. To do that we first query the most frequent n-grams from the training data. When dealing with fixed-text KD, for example, the features dimension is constant and constrained to the length of the typed text. This is not the case in free-text KD, where the text is unknown, and the feature dimension should handle every possible letter and number combination on the keyboard. Therefore, we use a limited size of the most common n-grams. The use of only a common set of n-grams speed up the algorithm work and decrease the needed memory and reduces the possibility of overfit.

3.4 Feature Extraction Example

To explain the final stage of the feature extraction, let's look at a simple example of the n-gram 'the', which appears twice in the text "The fast-paced athlete jumped over the hurdles effortlessly". The sequence of events for this n-gram is represented with $\downarrow$ for press and $\uparrow$ for release:

Occurrence 1: [($\downarrow$, "t", 6200), ($\uparrow$, "t", 6224), ($\downarrow$, "h", 6235), ($\uparrow$, "h", 6240), ($\downarrow$, "e", 6255), ($\uparrow$, "e", 6265)]

Occurrence 2: [($\downarrow$, "t", 7100), ($\uparrow$, "t", 7120), ($\downarrow$, "h", 7127), ($\uparrow$, "h", 7138), ($\downarrow$, "e", 7148), ($\uparrow$, "e", 7160)]

Table 1. Example's feature lists

Method	List
E2E	[65, 60]
EC	't': [24, 20]
–	'h': [5, 11]
–	'e': [10, 12]
RDT	'p_1': [24, 20]
–	'p_2': [5, 11]
–	'p_3': [10, 12]
AC	'p2r': [24, 5, 10, 20, 11, 12]
–	'r2p': [7, 10, 11, 15]
ACDT	[24, 5, 20, 10, 11, 12]
FDT	'p2r': [24, 20]
–	'r2p': [7, 11]
LD	'p2r': [10, 12]
–	'r2p': [10, 15]

Now we aggregate each one of our lists and perform our seven extraction methods on each one of them. Hence, our feature vector for each n-gram in the example is as in Table 1. Finally, the statistical features are extracted on each one of the lists of extraction and we receive a feature table we can vectorize such as in Table 2.

Table 2. Example's full feature table

Name	Mean	Std	Min	Max
E2E	62.5	2.5	60	65
EC_t	22	2	20	24
EC_h	8	3	5	11
EC_e	11	1	10	12
RDT_p_1	22	2	20	24
RDT_p_2	8	3	5	11
RDT_p_3	11	1	10	12
AC_p2r	13.66	6.39	5	24
AC_r2p	10.75	2.86	7	15
ACDT	13.66	6.39	5	24
FDT_p2r	22	2	20	24
FDT_r2p	9	2	7	11
LD_p2r	11	1	10	12
LD_r2p	12.5	2.5	10	15

3.5   Classifier

When dealing with free-text keystroke dynamics, one must take all possible desired features into consideration; even with the pick of the most common n-grams this creates many empty entries in each feature vector. Therefore, for the task of classification, we need a learning algorithm that can handle the relatively high dimensionality and sparsity of our feature space, as we had relatively low number of training samples for each user. For algorithms such as SVM and K-NN, this task might be difficult, however we tried them as well. Usually the number of features in free-text KD is relatively high. After testing several algorithms that were previously used, such as K-NN, SVM, MLP and tree-based algorithms such as random forest and gradient boosting, we decided to use the latter which gave the best results, specifically the XGBoost implementation [14].

Gradient boosting is a gradient descent-based algorithm that works with an ensemble of decision trees. The trees are built in a sequential way to find patterns in the residuals of the training data [12]. We chose XGBoost for the implementation because of its ability to handle missing values, which are often seen in high dimensionality feature spaces such as seen in free-text problems. One more advantage of XGBoost is its efficient implementation, which improves the computational time of the prediction and model creation.

4   Dataset

We used a public keystroke dynamics dataset called the Perez keystroke dataset, which is a superset of the "One-handed Keystroke Biometric Identification Competition" (OhKBIC) data [15]. The data collection was performed using three online exams taken by computer science bachelor's students on a web platform called Moodle, which is commonly used in universities. Each exam was composed from five essay questions. During the exam the students keystroke events were collected and sent to a server using JavaScript event logging framework. At the first exam the participants were instructed to use both hands to answer the questions (as they usually do), while at the second and third exams they were instructed to use only the left and right hand respectively.

In order to enforce the constraints of the second and third exams, approximately third of the exams conducted in classroom using standard desktop computers, where the rest of the students completed the exams on their personal devices which were a mix of desktop and laptop computers. To simulate real life usage as best as we could, we used only the two-handed exams subset of the dataset.

Eventually the dataset consists of data from 81 students, with at least 500 keystrokes on each exam for every student. We used the 66 out of the 81 that had relatively higher amount of data for our experiments. We used this dataset as it well represent the scenario of an attacker victim cooperation in cheating in remote exams.

5   Experiments and Results

The experiments were conducted based on an idea of *active and passive users*. The active users are used for building models and training them, and the passive users are only used for fraud testing purposes. We chose the 21 users with the highest amount of data to be the active users and the rest 45 to be the passive. We start by splitting the data of each active user into two: benign train and benign test with equally balanced size. For each active user we built a supervised model using his benign train data and fraud data which is randomly selected from the other active users training data. We tried to maintain a ratio of 1:10 in the training data for each user; each model was trained approximately on 35 user benign feature vectors and 350 fraud feature vectors. The passive users are then used in the evaluation of the models of the active users as test fraud sessions. The test set for each user is a combination of the user benign test data and the data of the passive users. For each user, the set-up of active users chosen for training and the passive users used for test were randomly changed to introduce variability in the experiments. The n-gram size used were of size $2 \leq n \leq 6$ as done by Sim et al. [17].

We performed several experiments on the dataset and evaluated the method with different algorithms and parameters. To evaluate the advantage of our method, we tested both our method (referred as extended n-graphs) and the current state of the art (referred as basic n-graphs) on known classifiers such as gradient boosting, random forest, SVM, K-NN and MLP.

An examination of the empirical results presented on Table 3 shows, as expected, when dealing with high dimensionality, K-NN and SVM did not perform well. We used K-NN in our experiment of with K = 5 which achieved AUC of 0.753, with an EER of 28% and SVM achieved almost random classification with an AUC of 0.58. Nevertheless, both algorithms performed better, with respect to AUC, using our method. Another algorithm previously used in the literature is MLP, the best result achieved with our method are 0.626 AUC and 37.3% EER while without it the results were much worse with 0.49 AUC and 50.7% EER. However, the ensemble tree-based algorithms performed much better. Random Forest (RF) with 100 trees produced an AUC of 0.83 with an EER of 22% using our method, in comparison to 0.787 AUC and 25.3% EER using the basic n-graphs. But the best performing algorithm was gradient boosting (XGB) used with 60 trees and learning rate of 0.15 gave the best classification results using our method with an AUC of 0.967 and an EER of 7.5%, and only 0.921 AUC and 12.4% EER using the basic-n-graphs.

Table 3. Classifiers EER and AUC of our method compared to the basic n-graphs

Classifier	AUC – basic n-graphs	AUC – extended n-graphs	EER – basic n-graphs	EER – extended n-graphs
XGB	0.921	0.967	12.4%	7.5%
RF	0.787	0.83	25.3%	22%
K-NN	0.5	0.753	50%	28%
MLP	0.492	0.626	50.7%	37.3%
SVM	0.463	0.58	53%	43%

As gradient boosting performed best, we deepen the examination in it. We started with researching the connection between the AUC and window size of feature vectors, comparing both basic n-graphs and our method.

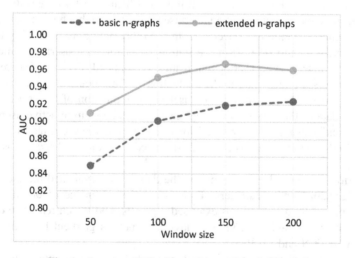

Fig. 1. Average AUC with respect to the window size

As showed in Fig. 1, for both methods the AUC is monotonically increasing as the size of the window grow, where its maximum lies at around 150 characters. Throughout the range of tested window sizes, our method performed better than the basic n-graphs, with an average AUC gap of 0.06.

Another interesting question we examined is what is the optimal number of common n-grams we need to include in our method. We performed an experiment with different numbers of common n-grams and compared the AUC results from our method.

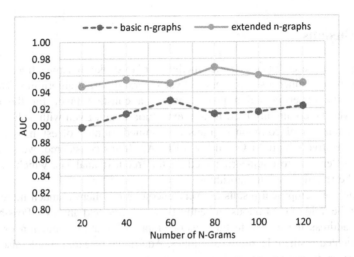

Fig. 2. Average AUC with respect to the number of selected n-grams

Figure 2 shows the AUC scores with respect to the number of common n-grams. Similar to the window size argument, the common n-grams also converged to a maximum point (from the range tested): around 80 common n-grams, with an AUC of 0.97.

In order to check the limitations of our method in terms of the size of the ensemble, we compared both methods AUC performance using gradient boosting with respect to the number of estimators.

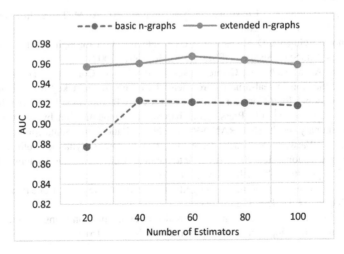

Fig. 3. Average AUC with respect to the number of estimators

As can be seen in Fig. 3. We have found that even with a relatively low number of only 20 estimators, the algorithm maintains almost the same performance level (which was not the case when we used the basic n-graphs) and remained superior given any tested number of estimators.

6 Conclusions

In this paper we presented an extended method for keystroke dynamics free text feature extraction and examined its performance over several different algorithms. The results throughout the experimentation phase showed a constant favor for the extended n-graphs over the commonly used feature extraction today. Even with a short window size, lower number of common n-grams and limited number of estimators we have achieved a relatively high AUC and low EER. All things considered, we successfully created a better feature engineering method for free-text analysis, which is superior given all the tested decision algorithms.

Although our empirical results are very encouraging, there is much more that can be done in the field of continuous authentication with free-text analysis. Possible future work can address the empty features using improved feature reduction or different sparsity oriented/resilient learning techniques. Additional research should also strive to obtain a larger dataset to test the improvements on a larger scale.

References

1. Shepherd, S.J.: Continuous authentication by analysis of keyboard typing characteristics. (1995)
2. Dowland, P.S., Furnell, S.M.: A long-term trial of keystroke profiling using digraph, trigraph and keyword latencies. In: Deswarte, Y., Cuppens, F., Jajodia, S., Wang, L. (eds.) SEC 2004. ITIFIP, vol. 147, pp. 275–289. Springer, Boston, MA (2004). https://doi.org/10.1007/1-4020-8143-X_18
3. Gunetti, D., Picardi, C.: Keystroke analysis of free text. ACM Trans. Inf. Syst. Secur. (TISSEC) 8(3), 312–347 (2005)
4. Bergadano, F., Gunetti, D., Picardi, C.: User authentication through keystroke dynamics. ACM Trans. Inf. Syst. Secur. (TISSEC) 5(4), 367–397 (2002)
5. Messerman, A., Mustafić, T., Camtepe, S.A., Albayrak, S.: Continuous and non-intrusive identity verification in real-time environments based on free-text keystroke dynamics. In: 2011 International Joint Conference on Biometrics (IJCB), pp. 1–8. IEEE, October 2011
6. Gaines, R.S., Lisowski, W., Press, S.J., Shapiro, N.: Authentication by keystroke timing: Some preliminary results (No. RAND-R-2526-NSF). Rand Corp, Santa Monica (1980)
7. Alsultan, A., Warwick, K.: User-friendly free-text keystroke dynamics authentication for practical applications. In: 2013 IEEE International Conference on Systems, Man, and Cybernetics, pp. 4658–4663. IEEE, October 2013
8. Ahmed, A.A., Traore, I.: Biometric recognition based on free-text keystroke dynamics. IEEE Trans. Cybern. 44(4), 458–472 (2013)
9. Kang, P., Cho, S.: Keystroke dynamics-based user authentication using long and free text strings from various input devices. Inf. Sci. 308, 72–93 (2015)

10. Ali, M.L., Tappert, C.C., Qiu, M., Monaco, J.V.: Authentication and identification methods used in keystroke biometric systems. In: 2015 IEEE 17th International Conference on High Performance Computing and Communications, 2015 IEEE 7th International Symposium on Cyberspace Safety and Security, and 2015 IEEE 12th International Conference on Embedded Software and Systems, pp. 1424–1429. IEEE, August 2015

11. Teh, P.S., Teoh, A.B.J., Yue, S.: A survey of keystroke dynamics biometrics. Sci. World J. (2013)

12. Friedman, J.H.: Greedy function approximation: a gradient boosting machine. Ann. Stat. **29**, 1189–1232 (2001)

13. Mondal, S., Bours, P.: Person identification by keystroke dynamics using pairwise user coupling. IEEE Trans. Inf. Forensics Secur. **12**(6), 1319–1329 (2017)

14. Chen, T., Guestrin, C.: XGBoost: a scalable tree boosting system. In: Proceedings of the 22nd ACM SIGKDD International Conference on Knowledge Discovery and Data Mining, pp. 785–794. ACM, August 2016

15. Monaco, J.V., et al.: One-handed keystroke biometric identification competition. In: 2015 International Conference on Biometrics (ICB), pp. 58–64. IEEE, May 2015

16. Shimshon, T., Moskovitch, R., Rokach, L., Elovici, Y.: Continuous verification using keystroke dynamics. In: 2010 International Conference on Computational Intelligence and Security, pp. 411–415. IEEE, December 2010

17. Sim, T., Janakiraman, R.: Are digraphs good for free-text keystroke dynamics? In: 2007 IEEE Conference on Computer Vision and Pattern Recognition. IEEE (2007)

Subversion-Resistant Commitment Schemes: Definitions and Constructions

Karim Baghery[1,2(✉)] (iD)

[1] imec-COSIC, KU Leuven, Leuven, Belgium
karim.baghery@kuleuven.be
[2] University of Tartu, Tartu, Estonia

Abstract. Recently, various news is reported about the subversion of *trusted* setup phase in mass-surveillance activities; strictly speaking about commitment schemes, recently it was discovered that the SwissPost-Scytl mix-net uses a trapdoor commitment scheme, that allows undetectably altering the votes and breaking users' privacy, given the trapdoor [Hae19,LPT19]. Motivated by such news and recent studies on subversion-resistance of various cryptographic primitives, this research studies the security of commitment schemes in the presence of a maliciously chosen commitment key. To attain a clear understanding of achievable security, we define a variety of current definitions called subversion hiding, subversion equivocality, and subversion binding. Then we provide both negative and positive results on constructing subversion-resistant commitment schemes, by showing that some combinations of notions are not compatible while presenting subversion-resistant constructions that can achieve other combinations.

Keywords: Commitment schemes · Subversion security · Reducing trust · CRS model

1 Introduction

The notion of commitment [Blu81] is one of the fundamental and widely used concepts in cryptography. A commitment scheme allows a committer to create a commitment c to a secret value of m, and later open the commitment c in a verifiable manner [GQ88,Ped92]. The procedure of generating c is called *committing* phase, and revealing or giving a proof-of-knowledge of message m and some secret information used in committing phase (precisely, randomnesses) called *opening*. In the Common Reference String (CRS) model, commitment schemes require a *setup* phase that is done by a trusted third party [CIO98], and it is shown that when we have a trusted setup phase, one-way functions are sufficient to construct Non-Interactive (NI) commitment schemes [Nao91,CIO98]. During last decades, we have seen various elegant NI commitment schemes that are deployed as a sub-protocol in wide range of cryptographic applications, to refer some, such as contract signing [EGL85], multi-party computation [GMW87], zero-knowledge

© Springer Nature Switzerland AG 2020
K. Markantonakis and M. Petrocchi (Eds.): STM 2020, LNCS 12386, pp. 106–122, 2020.
https://doi.org/10.1007/978-3-030-59817-4_7

proofs [GMW91, Dam90], e-voting [Gro05, Wik09], shuffle arguments [GL07] blockchains and their by-products (e.g. cryptocurrencies [BCG+14] and smart contracts [KMS+16]), and many other sensitive practical applications.

On the Security of Setup Phase. Along with developing various cryptographic primitives in sensitive applications, recently there have been various attacks or flaw reports on setup phase of cryptographic systems that rely on public parameters supposed to be generated honestly. In some cases, attacks are caused by maliciously (or incorrectly) generated public parameters or modifying cryptographic protocol specifications to embed backdoors, with intent to violate the security of the main system [BBG+13, PLS13, Gre14, Gab19, LPT19, Hae19]. Particularly about commitment schemes, recently two research [Hae19, LPT19] independently discovered that the implementation of shuffle argument in the SwissPost-Scytl mix-net uses a trapdoor commitment, which allows breaking security of the system without being detected. Indeed, the used commitment scheme has a trapdoor that having access to that, one can alter the votes or can break voters' privacy. So, given such a trapdoor, a malicious party can do an undetectable vote manipulation by an authority who sets up the mixing network[1].

Initiated by Bellare et al. [BPR14], recently subversion security has gotten considerable attention with focus on different cryptographic primitives including symmetric encryption schemes [BPR14], signature schemes [AMV15], non-interactive zero-knowledge proofs [BFS16, Bag19b], and public-key encryption schemes [ABK18]. Each of them considers achievable security in a particular family of primitives under subverted parameters. NI commitment schemes in the CRS model are another prominent family of primitives that require a trusted setup phase [Ped92, DF02, GOS06, Gro09, Gro10, Lip12]. As such commitment schemes are deployed in various areas of cryptography, so their security is not only important on itself but also security of other practical systems relies on it (e.g. guaranteeing the security of shuffling in mix-net of SwissPost-Scytl). Thus, their security under subverting public commitment key can have a crucial effect on the security of the bigger systems.

Our Contribution. We study the resistance of NI commitment schemes in the case of subverting commitment key and present definitions, negative results, along with some Subversion-Resistant (Sub-R) constructions as positive results. To get a clear understanding of achievable security, we first present new variations of current definitions, that are defined to guarantee the security of committers and verifiers even if the setup phase of a commitment scheme is subverted.

Recall that in the CRS model, an equivocal NI commitment scheme Π_{com} (e.g. [Gro10, Lip12]) is expected to satisfy, 1) Hiding: It is hard for any PPT adversary $\mathcal{A}$, given an honestly generated commitment key ck, to generate two messages $m_0 \neq m_1$ from message space $\mathcal{M}$ such that $\mathcal{A}$ can distinguish between their corresponding commitments c_0 and c_1 2) Binding: It is hard for any PPT

---

[1] More details in https://people.eng.unimelb.edu.au/vjteague/SwissVote and https://e-voting.bfh.ch/publications/2019/.

Table 1. Summary of results. Each row refers to achievability of selected notions.

| | Standard | | | Subversion resistant | | | |
	Hiding	Equivocal	Binding	Sub-hiding	Sub-equivocal	Sub-binding	Result in
Negative		✓				✓	Theorem 1
Positive 1	✓	✓	✓	✓	✓		Theorem 2
Positive 2	✓		✓	✓		✓	Theorem 3
Positive 3	✓	✓	✓	✓			Theorem 4

adversary $\mathcal{A}$, given an honestly generated commitment key ck, to come up with a collision $(c, m_0, \mathsf{op}_0, m_1, \mathsf{op}_1)$, such that op_0 and op_1 are valid opening values of two different pre-images $m_0 \neq m_1$ for c, 3) <u>Equivocality</u>: Given the trapdoor tk associated with ck, it is possible to create a fake commitment that can be opened successfully. Equivocality implies hiding, as a commitment is indistinguishable from an equivocal commitment which can be opened to any message.

Commitment Schemes with Subverted Parameters. We modify original definitions of commitments in [Gro09, Gro10, Lip12] and present a variation of them for Sub-R equivocal commitments. The key change in new definitions is that the adversary generates ck. When $\mathcal{A}$ generates ck, it can retain some trapdoors tk as a "backdoor" associated with ck. In Sect. 3.1, we formalize the following requirements for Sub-R commitments: 1) <u>Sub-hiding</u>: (subversion hiding) Even if a PPT $\mathcal{A}$ generates ck, if the ck is *well-formed*[2], it is hard for $\mathcal{A}$ to generate $m_0, m_1 \in \mathcal{M}$ s.t. $\mathcal{A}$ can distinguish between their corresponding commitments c_0 and c_1 where $(c_0, \mathsf{op}_0) \leftarrow \mathsf{Com}(\mathsf{ck}, m_0; r)$ and $(c_1, \mathsf{op}_1) \leftarrow \mathsf{Com}(\mathsf{ck}, m_1; r)$. 2) <u>Sub-binding</u>: (subversion binding) Even if a PPT $\mathcal{A}$ generates ck, if the ck is *well-formed*, it is hard for $\mathcal{A}$ to come up with a collision $(c, m_0, \mathsf{op}_0, m_1, \mathsf{op}_1)$, s.t. op_0 and op_1 are valid opening values of two different pre-images $m_0 \neq m_1$ for c. 3) <u>Sub-equivocality</u>: (subversion equivocality) Even if a PPT $\mathcal{A}$ generates ck, the scheme *still* should satisfy equivocality.

The relations between standard and new notions are shown in Fig. 1. Subversion-resistant variations imply the standard ones.

sub-equivocality $\longrightarrow$ sub-hiding		sub-binding	
$\downarrow$ $\quad$ $\downarrow$		$\downarrow$	
equivocality $\quad\longrightarrow\quad$ hiding		binding	

Fig. 1. Relation between current and new defined subversion-resistant notions.

Next, we consider how much subversion security is achievable in NI commitments. Our key results are summarized in Table 1. Each row considers constructing schemes that simultaneously can achieve the indicated notions (by ✓).

---

[2] Intuitively, the generated commitment key ck should have a well-defined structure.

Negative Result. We first consider whether we can achieve sub-binding along with the current notions, namely *sub-binding*, binding, hiding, and equivocality. The negative result in Table 1, indicates that we cannot achieve even standard equivocality and sub-binding at the same time. In Sect. 4, we show that achieving equivocality is in contradiction with achieving sub-binding.

Positive Results. Positive 1: By considering the negative result, the next best scenario would be the case that one can achieve all notions but sub-binding. In Theorem 2, we show that this case is possible, and we present a Sub-R commitment scheme that can achieve the notions indicated in the first positive result in Table 1. This result is established under the Bilinear Diffie-Hellman Knowledge of Exponents (BDH-KE) assumption, defined in Definition 2, and Γ-Power Symmetric Discrete Logarithm Assumption (Γ-PSDL), defined in Definition 1, assumptions in a group equipped with bilinear map. Positive 2: Next, we consider if there exists any practical commitment scheme that can achieve sub-binding. We already know from the negative result which sub-binding cannot be achieved by equivocality. Second positive result in Table 1 which is established in Theorem 3, shows that we can construct such commitment schemes. We show that basically this includes already known results that one can construct a hiding and binding commitment in the standard model. Positive 3: The third scenario is a commonly used case in practice. The scheme already satisfies hiding, equivocality, and binding and when we consider the case that keys are generated maliciously, it does not break completely, and indeed it still achieves hiding. In Sect. 5.3, we show that with minimal checks, Pedersen [Ped92] commitment scheme can achieve sub-hiding. This result might look redundant, as it is a restricted form of *Positive 1*, but this result is established entirely under standard assumptions.

In many cryptographic systems, it is shown the deployed commitment require equivocality, especially in minimizing the round complexity of zero-knowledge proofs [BFM88], or even constructing efficient NI zero-knowledge proofs [GS08, Gro10, Lip12]. A direct observation of the first positive result is that sub-equivocality can decrease the needed trust in such proof systems [Lip12].

On the Achievability of all Combinations. The main under focus question in this paper is for $X \in$ {hiding, binding, equivocality}, which combinations of X and sub-X are achievable at the same time. In Table 1, we only talked about four popular cases from 2^6 cases which one may think of. But one may notice that these four cases cover many of those cases. For instance, by considering relations between variations in Table 1, one may notice several trivial cases, and more importantly, the negative result covers a set of cases that are impossible to achieve. However, still, one can use a similar approach and go through over other cases and evaluate achievability of each one.

2   Preliminaries

Let $\lambda \in \mathbb{N}$ be the security parameter, and 1^λ denotes its unary representation; say $\lambda = 128$. $s \leftarrow_s S$ denotes picking s uniformly random from S. The empty string is shown with $\{\}$, e.g. ck = $\{\}$. For an algorithm $\mathcal{A}$, let im($\mathcal{A}$) be the image of $\mathcal{A}$, i.e., the set of valid outputs of $\mathcal{A}$, let RND($\mathcal{A}$) denote the random tape of $\mathcal{A}$, and let $r \leftarrow_{\$} $ RND($\mathcal{A}$) denote sampling of a randomizer r of sufficient length for $\mathcal{A}$'s needs. By $y \leftarrow \mathcal{A}(x; r)$ we denote the fact that $\mathcal{A}$, given an input x and a randomizer r, outputs y. Note that $\mathsf{Ext}_{\mathcal{A}}$ and $\mathcal{A}$ use internally the same randomness r. We denote by $\mathsf{negl}(\lambda)$ an arbitrary negligible function, and by $\mathsf{poly}(\lambda)$ an arbitrary polynomial function. For a tuple of integers $\Gamma = (\gamma_1, \ldots, \gamma_n)$ with $\gamma_i \leq \gamma_{i+1}$, let $(a_i)_{i \in \Gamma} = (a_{\gamma_1}, \ldots, a_{\gamma_n})$. We sometimes denote $(a_i)_{i \in [n]}$ as $\boldsymbol{a}$. We say that $\Gamma = (\gamma_1, \ldots, \gamma_n) \in \mathbb{Z}^n$ is an (n, λ)-nice tuple, if $0 \leq \gamma_1 \leq \cdots \leq \gamma_i \leq \gamma_n = \mathsf{poly}(\lambda)$. In games, $\Pr[G : y]$ shows the probability that y happens for the game G.

In pairing-based groups, we use additive notation together with the bracket notation, i.e., in group $\mathbb{G}_\mu$, $[a]_\mu = a[1]_\mu$, where $[1]_\mu$ is a fixed generator of $\mathbb{G}_\mu$. A *bilinear group generator* $\mathsf{BGgen}(1^\lambda)$ returns $(p, \mathbb{G}_1, \mathbb{G}_2, \mathbb{G}_T, \hat{e}, [1]_1, [1]_2)$, where p (a large prime) is the order of cyclic abelian groups $\mathbb{G}_1$, $\mathbb{G}_2$, and $\mathbb{G}_T$. Finally, $\hat{e} : \mathbb{G}_1 \times \mathbb{G}_2 \rightarrow \mathbb{G}_T$ is an efficient non-degenerate bilinear pairing, s.t. $\hat{e}([a]_1, [b]_2) = [ab]_T$. Denote $[a]_1 \bullet [b]_2 = \hat{e}([a]_1, [b]_2)$.

Definition 1 (Γ-Power (Symmetric) Discrete Logarithm Assumption). *Let Γ be an (n, λ)-nice tuple for some $n = \mathsf{poly}(\lambda)$. We say a bilinear group generator BGgen is (n, λ)-PDL secure in group $\mathbb{G}_t$ for $t \in \{1, 2\}$, if for any PPT adversary A, $\Pr[\mathsf{gk} := (p, \mathbb{G}_1, \mathbb{G}_2, \mathbb{G}_T, \hat{e}, [1]_1, [1]_2) \leftarrow \mathsf{BGgen}(1^\lambda), [1]_t \leftarrow \mathbb{G}_t \backslash \{1\}, x \leftarrow \mathbb{Z}_p : \mathcal{A}(\mathsf{gk}; ([x^l]_t)_{l \in \Gamma})]$ is negligible in λ. Similarly, we say a bilinear group generator BGgen is Γ-PSDL secure, if for any PPT adversary $\mathcal{A}$,*

$$\Pr\left[\begin{array}{l} \mathsf{gk} := (p, \mathbb{G}_1, \mathbb{G}_2, \mathbb{G}_T, \hat{e}, [1]_1, [1]_2) \leftarrow \mathsf{BGgen}(1^\lambda), \\ x \leftarrow \mathbb{Z}_p : \mathcal{A}(\mathsf{gk}, ([x^l]_1, [x^l]_2)_{l \in \Gamma}) = x \end{array}\right] = \mathsf{negl}(\lambda).$$

Lipmaa [Lip12] has proven that the Γ-PSDL assumption holds in the generic group model for any (n, λ)-nice tuple Γ given $n = poly(\lambda)$.

Definition 2 (BDH-KE Assumption). *We say BGgen is BDH-KE secure for $\mathcal{R}$ if for any λ, $(\mathbf{R}, \xi_{\mathbf{R}}) \in \mathsf{im}(\mathcal{R}(1^\lambda))$, and PPT adversary $\mathcal{A}$ there exists a PPT extractor $\mathsf{Ext}_{\mathcal{A}}$, such that*

$$\mathsf{Adv}_{\mathsf{BGgen}, \mathcal{A}, \mathsf{Ext}_{\mathcal{A}}}^{BDH-KE} = \Pr\left[\begin{array}{l} (p, \mathbb{G}_1, \mathbb{G}_2, \mathbb{G}_T, \hat{e}, [1]_1, [1]_2) \leftarrow \mathsf{BGgen}(1^\lambda), r \leftarrow_{\$} \mathsf{RND}(\mathcal{A}), \\ ([\alpha_1]_1, [\alpha_2]_2 \| a) \leftarrow (\mathcal{A} \| \mathsf{Ext}_{\mathcal{A}})(\mathbf{R}, \xi_{\mathbf{R}}; r) : \\ [\alpha_1]_1 \bullet [1]_2 = [1]_1 \bullet [\alpha_2]_2 \wedge a \neq \alpha_1 \end{array}\right]$$

is negligible in λ. In above assumption, $\xi_{\mathbf{R}}$ is the auxiliary information related to the underlying group. This is an asymmetric-pairing version of the original knowledge assumption [Dam92].

3 Security of Commitments Under Parameters Subversion

Let Setup be a setup algorithm that takes as input λ and outputs some setup information $\mathsf{gk} \leftarrow \mathsf{Setup}(1^\lambda)$. In the basic form, a NI commitment scheme consists of a tuple of polynomial-time algorithms (KGen, Com, Ver). We consider equivocal commitments (a.k.a. trapdoor commitments) that consists of algorithms (KGen, Com, Ver, KGen*, Com*, Equiv). KGen is a PPT algorithm that given gk generates a ck and a trapdoor key tk. As in [Gro09], the gk can describe a finite group over which we are working, or simply the security parameter. We assume all parties have access to gk. Com takes ck, a message m, a randomizer r and outputs c and an opening op. Given ck, c, m and op, Ver returns either 1 or 0. In equivocal commitments, given tk, it is possible to open a c to any message. This property is formalized by PPT algorithms Com* and Equiv, where Com* takes tk (generated by KGen*) and outputs an equivocal commitment c and an equivocation key ek. Then, Equiv on inputs ek, c and a message m creates an opening op $:= r$ of c, so that $(c, \text{op}) = \text{Com}(\text{ck}, m; r)$. Here, we define Sub-R equivocal commitment schemes and add a new algorithm CKVer to the scheme that will be used to verify the well-formedness of ck.

Definition 3 (Subversion-resistant Equivocal Commitments). *A Sub-R equivocal commitment scheme consists of eight algorithms defined as below,*

Key Generation, ck $\leftarrow$ KGen(gk): *Generates a commitment key* ck *and associated trapdoor* tk. *It also specifies a message space* $\mathcal{M}$, *a randomness space* $\mathcal{R}$, *and a commitment space* $\mathcal{C}$.

Commitment Key Verification, $0/1 \leftarrow$ CKVer(gk, ck): CKVer *is a deterministic algorithm that given* gk *and* ck, *returns either 1 or 0;*

Committing, $(c, \text{op}) \leftarrow$ Com(ck, $m; r$): *Outputs a* c *and an opening* op. *It specifies a function* Com $: \mathcal{M} \times \mathcal{R} \rightarrow \mathcal{C}$. *Given a* $m \in \mathcal{M}$, *the committer picks an* $r \in \mathcal{R}$ *and computes the* $(c, \text{op}) = \text{Com}(\text{ck}, m; r)$.

Opening Verification, $0/1 \leftarrow$ Ver(ck, c, m, op): *Outputs 1 if* $m \in \mathcal{M}$ *is the committed message in* c *with opening* op, *and returns 0 otherwise.*

Simulation of Key Generation, $(\text{ck}, \text{tk}) \leftarrow$ KGen*(gk): *Generates a key* ck *and associated trapdoor* tk. *It also specifies spaces* $\mathcal{M}$, $\mathcal{R}$, *and* $\mathcal{C}$.

Trapdoor Committing, $(c, \text{ek}) \leftarrow$ Com*(ck, tk): *Given* ck *and* tk *as input, outputs an equivocal commitment* c *and an equivocation key* ek.

Trapdoor Opening, op $\leftarrow$ Equiv(ek, c, m, ek): *On inputs* ek, c *and an* m *creates an opening* op $:= r$ *of* c, *s.t.* $(c, \text{op}) = \text{Com}(\text{ck}, m; r)$ *and returns* op.

A (subversion-resistant) commitment scheme satisfies *completeness* if for ck $\leftarrow$ KGen(gk) and any honestly generated commitment of $m \in \mathcal{M}$, it successfully passes the verification, i.e., Ver(ck, Com(ck, m; op), m, op) = 1.

3.1 Notions for Commitments with Subverted Parameters

Due to the lack of space, definitions of standard notions for equivocal commitments are provided in the full version [Bag19a]. In the standard notions, the commitment key ck is honestly generated by a trusted third party. But as our goal is to consider achievable security when the setup phase is compromised, so we cannot assume such assumption and instead we define subversion-resistance analogues sub-hiding, sub-equivocality and sub-binding of the notions hiding, equivocality and binding. In new notions, the key difference is that the setup is compromised and ck is generated by an adversary (or a subverter) rather than via the honest algorithm KGen prescribed by Π_{com}. Also, in Sub-R commitments there is a new algorithm CKVer to verify well-formedness of ck.

In the following definitions, let Setup be an algorithm that takes as input the security parameter λ and outputs some setup information $gk \leftarrow Setup(1^\lambda)$.

Definition 4 (Subversion Hiding (Sub-Hiding)). *A commitment scheme Π_{com} satisfies computationally subversion hiding if for any PPT adversary $\mathcal{A}$,*

$$\left| 2\Pr\left[\begin{array}{l} (ck, (m_0, m_1)) \leftarrow \mathcal{A}(gk), b \leftarrow_s \{0,1\}, \mathsf{CKVer}(gk, ck) = 1, \\ r_b \leftarrow_s \mathcal{R}, (c_b, op_b) \leftarrow \mathsf{Com}(ck, m_b; r_b), b' \leftarrow \mathcal{A}(c_b) : b' = b \end{array} \right] - 1 \right| = \mathsf{negl}(\lambda).$$

The scheme is perfectly subversion hiding if the above probability is equal to 0.

By *well-formedness* of ck we mean the CKVer will verify ck successfully.

Definition 5 (Subversion Binding (Sub-Binding)). *A commitment scheme Π_{com} satisfies computationally subversion binding if for any PPT $\mathcal{A}$,*

$$\Pr\left[\begin{array}{l} (ck, c, (m_0, op_0), (m_1, op_1)) \leftarrow \mathcal{A}(gk) : \mathsf{CKVer}(gk, ck) = 1 \wedge \\ (m_0 \neq m_1) \wedge (\mathsf{Ver}(ck, c, m_0, op_0) = 1) \wedge (\mathsf{Ver}(ck, c, m_1, op_1) = 1) \end{array} \right] = \mathsf{negl}(\lambda).$$

The commitment is perfectly subversion binding if the probability is equal to 0.

Intuitively, *subversion binding* states that an adversary $\mathcal{A}$ will not be able to do double open a commitment c, even if it generates the (well-formed) key ck.

Definition 6 (Subversion Equivocality (Sub-Equivocality)). *A commitment scheme Π_{com} satisfies subversion equivocalability if for any PPT $\mathcal{A}$,*

$$\left| \Pr\left[\begin{array}{l} (ck, m) \leftarrow \mathcal{A}(gk), r \leftarrow_s \mathcal{R}, \\ (c, op) \leftarrow \mathsf{Com}(ck, m; r) : \\ \mathcal{A}(ck, c, op) = 1 \wedge \\ \mathsf{CKVer}(gk, ck) = 1 \end{array} \right] - \Pr\left[\begin{array}{l} (ck, tk) \leftarrow \mathsf{KGen}^*(gk), m \leftarrow \mathcal{M} \\ (c, ek) \leftarrow \mathsf{Com}^*(ck, tk), \\ op \leftarrow \mathsf{Equiv}(ek, c, m) : \\ \mathcal{A}(ck, c, op) = 1 \wedge \\ \mathsf{CKVer}(gk, ck) = 1, \end{array} \right] \right| \leq \mathsf{negl}(\lambda),$$

where $\mathcal{A}$ outputs $m \in \mathcal{M}$ and KGen^* is a key generator which also returns tk.

Intuitively, subversion equivocality states that even if $\mathcal{A}$ (a malicious key generator) generates the ck, still the scheme satisfies equivocality. One may notice that sub-equivocality implies sub-hiding and standard equivocality.

Lemma 1. *A commitment scheme that satisfies a security notion with subvertible setup also satisfies the security notion with honest setup.*

Proof. To prove the lemma, we show that an adversary $\mathcal{A}$ against an honest setup can be used to construct an adversary $\mathcal{B}$ against a subvertible setup.

Adversary $\mathcal{B}$ first samples a ck honestly, i.e., $ck \leftarrow \mathsf{KGen}(gk)$ and checks that $\mathsf{CKVer}(gk, ck) = 1$. Next, sends ck to $\mathcal{A}$ and gets the answer and sends it to the challenger. Similarly, follows the rest of experiment and wins the game of subversion security with the same probability as $\mathcal{A}$ wins the standard game.   □

4 Sub-binding with Equivocability Are Not Compatible

In this section, we consider if we can achieve sub-binding without degrading hiding, binding, equivocality. Achieving sub-binding individually is possible (e.g. by sending a plain message) but such a scheme will not guarantee equivocality. Here we consider the practically-interested cases. We first consider the achievability of sub-binding and (sub-)equivocality at the same time. We show that achieving simultaneously sub-binding and (even) standard equivocality is impossible.

Theorem 1 (Impossibility of Sub-binding along with Equivocality).
There cannot exists a CRS-based commitment scheme Π_{com} = (KGen, CKVer, Com, Ver, KGen*, Com*, Equiv) which can satisfy equivocality and sub-binding at the same time.

Proof. Sketch. The definition of equivocality (in the full version [Bag19a]) states that there exists KGen* that given gk returns (ck, tk), and given trapdoor tk there exist two algorithms Com* and Equiv that allow one to create a fake commitment and a valid opening which are indistinguishable from an honestly generated commitment and opening. So, given those algorithms, an adversary of sub-binding can first generate ck and tk honestly. Then, it gives ck and tk as input to Com* and calculates $(c, ek) \leftarrow$ Com*(ck, tk). After that, it samples $(m_0, m_1) \in \mathcal{M}$, where $m_0 \neq m_1$ and invokes the algorithm Equiv twice for two different messages, and generates $op_0 \leftarrow$ Equiv(ek, c, m_0) and $op_1 \leftarrow$ Equiv(ek, c, m_1) and sends $(c, (m_0, op_0), (m_1, op_1))$ to the challenger of sub-binding game and wins with probability 1, as each of the tuples (m_0, op_0) and (m_1, op_1) are a (distinct) valid opening for c. On the other hand, sub-binding requires that $\mathcal{A}$ should not be able to double open even if he generates the ck. But, one can observe that achieving equivocality implies that given tk one can use Com* and Equiv and generate two valid opening with different messages which will break sub-binding.

That was the key idea behind the proof, and the full proof is provided in the full version [Bag19a].   □

5 Positive Results

Next, we consider if we can construct subversion-resistant commitment schemes in the CRS model, which without losing current security guarantees will achieve some of the subversion-resistant notions defined in Sect. 3.1. For instance, can we achieve sub-equivocality without losing the initial properties? We answer this question positively in Subsect. 5.1, by introducing a commitment scheme in the CRS model that can achieve sub-equivocality and binding. By considering the negative result, this is the best case one can achieve if they want to retain equivocality when commitment key is subverted. In the second scenario, we consider if we can construct commitment schemes that will satisfy sub-binding? In Subsect. 5.2, we show the best we can achieve while retaining sub-binding is sub-hiding; by introducing some already known schemes that simultaneously achieving sub-binding and sub-hiding. The first positive result provides sub-equivocality and binding under a knowledge assumption. One may ask, can we relax the requirement of sub-equivocality and aim to retain sub-hiding but from weaker assumptions? This is answered positively in Subsect. 5.3.

5.1   Sub-equivocality and Binding

By considering the definition of sub-equivocality (given in Definition 6), to achieve sub-equivocality in a commitment scheme, there must be algorithms KGen*, Com* and Equiv, where KGen* simulates *malicious* setup phase, and Com* and Equiv output a fake commitment and the associated valid opening, consequently. In this case, the algorithms Com* and Equiv cannot get honestly generated trapdoors of ck, and they cannot extract the trapdoors from the malicious key generator $\mathcal{A}$ by rewinding, as they do not have any interaction with $\mathcal{A}$. So instead, we will rely on a knowledge assumption, which allows extracting trapdoors of ck from a malicious key generator in a non-black-box way. Once we extracted the tk, it will be provided to algorithms Com* and Equiv to generate a pair of fake but acceptable commitment and opening. Moreover, in the case of a malicious key generator, there is an issue with the setup information gk, e.g. groups description. They cannot be generated as before, as they can be subverted. Similar to subversion-resistant NIZK arguments [BFS16], this issue is addressed by considering the gk as a part of the scheme specification. More precisely, since group generation is a deterministic and public procedure, so in subversion-resistant commitment schemes, all parties will re-execute group generation themselves to obtain gk. To guarantee binding, the minimal requirement is that an adversary cannot obtain the tk of ck from a honestly generated ck.

Theorem 2 (A Sub-equivocal and Binding Commitment). *Let* BGgen *be a bilinear group generator. Then the commitment scheme* Π_{com} *described in Fig. 2 which is a variation of knowledge commitment scheme introduced in [Gro10, Lip12], is binding in* $\mathbb{G}_t$ *for* $t \in \{1, 2\}$, *under the* Γ-PDL *assumption and also satisfies sub-equivocality under the BDH-KE knowledge assumption.*

Proof. Our proposed variation has the same ck as the original scheme, so the proof of (knowledge) binding can be shown straightforwardly from the original scheme, which is done in [Lip12] under the Γ-PSDL assumption in the group $\mathbb{G}_t$ for $t \in \{1, 2\}$.

To prove sub-equivocality, it was shown that the original scheme is equivocal under a trusted setup, namely the setup phase is simulatable, and the algorithms Com* and Equiv that can generate a fake commitment and valid opening are shown in Fig. 2. In the original scheme, the algorithms Com* and Equiv get the honestly generated trapdoor tk, but in our case the tk is not trustable anymore.

Let $\mathcal{A}$ be a malicious key generator. To prove sub-equivocality, we first need to show that the setup phase is simulatable. Namely, there exists KGen* which can produce the full view of key generation by $\mathcal{A}$. Second, we need to describe

---

Setup, gk ← BGgen(1^λ): Given 1^λ, return gk $:= (p, \mathbb{G}_1, \mathbb{G}_2, \mathbb{G}_T, \hat{e}, [1]_1, [1]_2)$, where
  p (a large prime) is the order of cyclic Abelian groups $\mathbb{G}_1$, $\mathbb{G}_2$, and $\mathbb{G}_T$; $\hat{e}$:
  $\mathbb{G}_1 \times \mathbb{G}_2 \to \mathbb{G}_T$ is an efficient non-degenerate bilinear pairing.

Key Generation, ck ← KGen(gk): Let Γ be an (n, λ)-nice tuple for some $n =$
  poly(λ) with $\gamma_i = i$ in the original version, for $i \in [0..n]$. Sample $\hat{a}, x \leftarrow \mathbb{Z}_p$.
  Let $t \in \{1, 2\}$. Return the key ck $= (\text{ck}_1, \text{ck}_2)$ where $\text{ck}_t \leftarrow \{[x^i]_t, [\hat{a}x^i]_t\}$ for
  $i \in [0..n]$ and the corresponding trapdoor tk as tk $= x$.

Commitment Key Verification, 0/1 ← CKVer(gk, ck): Given gk and the com-
  mitment key ck, first parse $ck := (\{[x^i]_1, [\hat{a}x^i]_1\}, \{[x^i]_2, [\hat{a}x^i]_2\})$ for $i \in [0..n]$
  and then do the following verification on elements of the ck,
  - Check whether $[\hat{a}]_1 \bullet [1]_2 = [1]_1 \bullet [\hat{a}]_2$
  - For $i \in [1..n]$ check:
    1. $[x^i]_1 \bullet [1]_2 = [1]_1 \bullet [x^i]_2$
    2. $[\hat{a}x^i]_1 \bullet [1]_2 = [1]_1 \bullet [\hat{a}x^i]_2$
    3. $[\hat{a}]_1 \bullet [x^i]_2 = [1]_1 \bullet [\hat{a}x^i]_2$
    4. $[\hat{a}x]_1 \bullet [x^{i-1}]_2 = [1]_1 \bullet [\hat{a}x^i]_2$
  and return 1 if all checks passed successfully; otherwise return 0.

Committing, $(c, \text{op}) \leftarrow$ Com(ck, m; r): Given (ck, m) for CKVer(gk, ck) $= 1$, to
  commit to $m = (m_1, m_2, \ldots, m_n) \in \mathbb{Z}_p^n$ sample a random $r \leftarrow_s \mathbb{Z}_p$, and return
  $(c, \text{op} := r)$ that are defined as follows,

$$c := (c_t^1, c_t^2) = (r[1]_t + \textstyle\sum_{i=1}^n m_i [x^i]_t, r[\hat{a}]_t + \textstyle\sum_{i=1}^n m_i [\hat{a}x^i]_t)$$

Opening Verification, 0/1 ← Ver(ck, c, m, op): Given c, m and op $= r$, recompute
  c as original one and check if it is equal to given c and return 0/1.

Simulation of Key Generation, (ck, tk) ← KGen*(gk): Use the simulation algorithm Sim$\mathcal{A}$ in Fig. 4 and generates a key pair (ck, tk $:= (x, \hat{a})$).

Trapdoor Committing, $(c, \text{ek}) \leftarrow$ Com*(ck, tk): Given the a key pair (ck, tk),
  output an equivocal commitment $c = [r]_t$ where $r \leftarrow \mathbb{Z}_p^2$ and an equivocation
  key ek $= (\text{tk}, r)$.

Trapdoor Opening, op ← Equiv(ek, c, m): On input equivocation key ek $= (\text{tk} :=$
  $(x, \hat{a}), r \in \mathbb{Z}_p^2), c \in \mathcal{C}^2$ and messages m create an opening $r' = r - \sum_{i=1}^n m_i x^i)$ for
  any m, so that $(c, \text{op}) = $ Com(ck, a; r') and return op $= r'$.

Fig. 2. A variation of the commitment scheme of Groth [Gro10] defined by Lipmaa [Lip12] that achieves sub-equivocality and binding. We note that in this setting,
gk $:= (p, \mathbb{G}_1, \mathbb{G}_2, \mathbb{G}_T, \hat{e}, [1]_1, [1]_2)$ is part of the scheme specification, and in practice
each party can run deterministic algorithm BGgen and re-obtain gk.

two algorithms Com* and Equiv which given the extracted trapdoor they can
produce a fake commitment and a valid opening which are indistinguishable
from the real ones. To address the first issue, we construct a non-black-box
extraction algorithm Ext$_\mathcal{A}$ that can extract the trapdoor tk from a malicious key
generator $\mathcal{A}$ and simulate the setup phase. Recall that the BDH-KE assumption
for bilinear groups $\mathbb{G}_1$ and $\mathbb{G}_2$ generated by $[1]_1$ and $[1]_2$, respectively, states that

---

Extraction algorithm, tk ← Ext$_{\mathcal{A}}$(gk, ck, $\xi_\mathbf{R}$):

Given source code and random coins of the malicious key generator $\mathcal{A}$, and some auxiliary information $\xi_\mathbf{R}$ it extracts $(x, \hat{a})$ ← Ext$_{\mathcal{A}}$(gk, ck, $\xi_\mathbf{R}$) and set tk := $(x, \hat{a})$; Finally, **Return** tk.

Fig. 3. A BDH-KE assumption based extraction algorithm Ext$_{\mathcal{A}}$ for the sub-equivocal commitment scheme described in Fig. 2

Simulator Sim$\mathcal{A}$(gk) :

gk := $(p, \mathbb{G}_1, \mathbb{G}_2, \mathbb{G}_T, \hat{e}, [1]_1, [1]_2, \xi_\mathbf{R})$ ← BGgen(1^λ); ck ← $\mathcal{A}$(gk);   # as in Fig. 2
By executing CKVer(gk, ck),
    Check whether $[\hat{a}]_1 \bullet [1]_2 = [1]_1 \bullet [\hat{a}]_2$
    For $i \in [1 .. n]$ check:
    1. $[x^i]_1 \bullet [1]_2 = [1]_1 \bullet [x^i]_2$
    2. $[\hat{a}x^i]_1 \bullet [1]_2 = [1]_1 \bullet [\hat{a}x^i]_2$
    3. $[\hat{a}]_1 \bullet [x^i]_2 = [1]_1 \bullet [\hat{a}x^i]_2$
    4. $[\hat{a}x]_1 \bullet [x^{i-1}]_2 = [1]_1 \bullet [\hat{a}x^i]_2$
    if the checks pass, tk := $(x, \hat{a})$ ← Ext$_{\mathcal{A}}$(gk, ck, $\xi_\mathbf{R}$)   # as in Fig. 3
    Otherwise tk ← $\perp$
Return (ck, tk)

Fig. 4. Simulation of the setup phase in the knowledge commitment scheme described in Fig. 2.

from any algorithm, given the group description and generators, which returns a pair $([a]_1, [a]_2)$, one can efficiently extracts a. In the rest of the proof, we construct an efficient extractor under BDH-KE assumption which allows us to extract the trapdoor td from $\mathcal{A}$.

Let $\mathcal{A}$ outputs ck = (ck_1, ck_2), where ck_t ← $\{[x^i]_t, [\hat{a}x^i]_t\}$ for $i \in [0 .. n]$ and $t \in \{1, 2\}$, as described in Fig. 2. By considering BDH-KE assumption, and verifications done in CKVer, one can observe that if a malicious key generator $\mathcal{A}$ manages to output a *well-formed* ck, it must know x and $\hat{a}$. By well-formed ck, we mean it must pass all checks in CKVer[3]. So it implies that there exists a polynomial time extractor Ext$_{\mathcal{A}}$ that if all the verifications in CKVer pass for some $\hat{a}$ and x, then the Ext$_{\mathcal{A}}$ can extracts x and $\hat{a}$; as Adv$^{BDH-KE}_{BGgen,\mathcal{A},Ext_{\mathcal{A}}}$ is negligible. A high-level description of the extraction procedure is shown in Fig. 3. After using the extractor Ext$_{\mathcal{A}}$, one can simulate a malicious key generation using algorithm Sim$\mathcal{A}$ described in Fig. 4.

---

[3] Note that verifications such as $[\hat{a}]_1 \bullet [1]_2 = [1]_1 \bullet [\hat{a}]_2$ inside CKVer comes from the definition of the BDH-KE. So to check the well-formedness of commitment key ck, depending on the underlying knowledge assumption in different commitment schemes, one may construct a CKVer algorithm with different verification equations.

Batched Commitment Key Verification, $0/1 \leftarrow$ CKVer(gk, ck): Batched CKVer is an efficient algorithm that given commitment key ck and public setup information gk (that can be computed locally), does the following verifications on ck elements,

- Parse or recompute $gk := (p, \mathbb{G}_1, \mathbb{G}_2, \mathbb{G}_T, \hat{e}, [1]_1, [1]_2) \leftarrow$ BGgen(1^λ);
- Samples three vector of randomnesses with length n as $\boldsymbol{r}, \boldsymbol{s}, \boldsymbol{t}, \boldsymbol{q} \leftarrow_\$ \{1, \ldots, 2^\lambda\}$;
- If $\left([\hat{a}]_1 + \sum_{i=1}^n r_i [x^i]_1 + \sum_{i=1}^n s_i [\hat{a}x^i]_1\right) \bullet [1]_2 + [\hat{a}]_1 \bullet$ $\sum_{i=1}^n t_i [x^i]_2 + [\hat{a}x]_1 \bullet \sum_{i=1}^n q_i [x^{i-1}]_2 = [1]_1 \bullet$ $\left([\hat{a}]_2 + \sum_{i=1}^n r_i [x^i]_2 + \sum_{i=1}^n s_i [\hat{a}x^i]_2 + \sum_{i=1}^n t_i [\hat{a}x^i]_2 + \sum_{i=1}^n q_i [\hat{a}x^i]_2\right),$ then **return** 1 (the ck is well-formed);
- Else, **return** 0 (the ck is not well-formed);

Fig. 5. Batched CKVer algorithm for sub-equivocal commitment scheme in Fig. 2

Finally, using the extracted trapdoor tk, one can consider the rest of proof as the proof of equivocality given in the original scheme [Lip12], by showing that given the (extracted) trapdoors one can use two algorithms Com* and Equiv (described in Fig. 2) and generate a fake commitment and the corresponding valid opening that will be successfully verified by Ver. □

Remark 1. In practice, executing the CKVer algorithm on long commitment keys might take considerable time. In such cases, to make CKVer more efficient, one can use batching techniques [BGR98, HHK+17] to speed up the verification.

Below, we proposed a batched version of the proposed CKVer. For the sub-equivocal commitment scheme given in Fig. 2, to execute CKVer, one needs to compute $6n + 2$ parings (note that right hand of some verifications are the same). But with batched CKVer algorithm in Fig. 5, one can verify ck with only 4 parings and $8n$ exponentiations, that for large values of n, this takes considerably less time. This can also be optimized by using the same randomness for the different equations, that would allow to save $2n$ exponentiations.

5.2 Sub-binding and Sub-hiding

Next, we discuss the second positive result. Let $\Pi_{com}^{2-party} = (\text{KGen}, \text{Com}, \text{Ver})$ be a commitment that does not require a particular setup and the output of KGen can be ignored. This includes all classical commitments that guarantee hiding and binding and do not require a setup. In other words, all the commitments that only need to choose some public parameters that can be agreed between both parties, e.g., agreeing on the order and generator of the underlying group or a particular secure and collision resistant hash function family.

We show that such hiding and binding commitment schemes also guarantee sub-hiding and sub-binding. Intuitively, one can see that in such case (e.g. ck = {}) there is no risk of subverting ck.

Lemma 2. *Let $\Pi_{com}^{2-party}$ = (KGen, Com, Ver) be a commitment scheme that does not require a particular setup phase. If $\Pi_{com}^{2-party}$ satisfies binding and hiding, it also guarantees sub-binding and sub-hiding.*

Proof. Let $\mathcal{A}$ be a sub-binding adversary, meaning that

$$\Pr\left[\begin{array}{l} \mathsf{gk} \leftarrow \mathsf{Setup}(1^\lambda), (\mathsf{ck}, c, (m_0, \mathsf{op}_0), (m_1, \mathsf{op}_1)) \leftarrow \mathcal{A}(\mathsf{gk}): \\ \mathsf{CKVer}(\mathsf{gk}, \mathsf{ck}) = 1 \wedge (m_0 \neq m_1) \\ \wedge (\mathsf{Ver}(\mathsf{ck}, c, m_0, \mathsf{op}_0) = 1) \wedge (\mathsf{Ver}(\mathsf{ck}, c, m_1, \mathsf{op}_1) = 1) \end{array}\right] = 1 - \mathsf{negl}(\lambda).$$

By considering the fact that in a $\Pi_{com}^{2-party}$ commitment, so its commitment key can be generated by either $\mathcal{A}$ or the honest KGen. So in above game, one can substitute malicious key generator $\mathcal{A}$ with an honest KGen, meaning that

$$\Pr\left[\begin{array}{l} \mathsf{gk} \leftarrow \mathsf{Setup}(1^\lambda), \mathsf{ck} \leftarrow \mathsf{KGen}(\mathsf{gk}), \\ (c, (m_0, \mathsf{op}_0), (m_1, \mathsf{op}_1)) \leftarrow \mathcal{A}(\mathsf{gk}, \mathsf{ck}): \mathsf{CKVer}(\mathsf{gk}, \mathsf{ck}) = 1 \wedge \\ (m_0 \neq m_1) \wedge (\mathsf{Ver}(\mathsf{ck}, c, m_0, \mathsf{op}_0) = 1) \wedge (\mathsf{Ver}(\mathsf{ck}, c, m_1, \mathsf{op}_1) = 1) \end{array}\right] = 1 - \mathsf{negl}(\lambda).$$

which gives us a new successful adversary for binding of the commitment scheme $\Pi_{com}^{2-party}$. As a result, if $\Pi_{com}^{2-party}$ guarantees binding, so it is also sub-binding.

Similarly, let $\mathcal{A}$ be a sub-hiding adversary, meaning that

$$\left|2\Pr\left[\begin{array}{l} \mathsf{gk} \leftarrow \mathsf{Setup}(1^\lambda), (\mathsf{ck}, (m_0, m_1)) \leftarrow \mathcal{A}(\mathsf{gk}), \\ b \leftarrow_\$ \{0, 1\}, \mathsf{CKVer}(\mathsf{gk}, \mathsf{ck}) = 1, r_b \leftarrow_\$ \mathcal{R}, \\ (c_b, \mathsf{op}_b) \leftarrow \mathsf{Com}(\mathsf{ck}, m_b; r_b), b' \leftarrow \mathcal{A}(c_b): b' = b \end{array}\right] - 1\right| = 1 - \mathsf{negl}(\lambda).$$

Again, by considering the property of a $\Pi_{com}^{2-party}$ commitment, one can substitute malicious key generator $\mathcal{A}$ in the setup phase with an honest KGen, which results,

$$\left|2\Pr\left[\begin{array}{l} \mathsf{gk} \leftarrow \mathsf{Setup}(1^\lambda), \mathsf{ck} \leftarrow \mathsf{KGen}(\mathsf{gk}), (m_0, m_1) \leftarrow \mathcal{A}(\mathsf{gk}), \\ b \leftarrow_\$ \{0, 1\}, \mathsf{CKVer}(\mathsf{gk}, \mathsf{ck}) = 1, r_b \leftarrow_\$ \mathcal{R}, \\ (c_b, \mathsf{op}_b) \leftarrow \mathsf{Com}(\mathsf{ck}, m_b; r_b), b' \leftarrow \mathcal{A}(c_b): b' = b \end{array}\right] - 1\right| = 1 - \mathsf{negl}(\lambda).$$

that gives us a new successful adversary for hiding of the commitment scheme $\Pi_{com}^{2-party}$. Hence, if $\Pi_{com}^{2-party}$ guarantees binding, so it is also sub-binding. Note that when the key generation is done honestly, CKVer always returns 1.   □

Theorem 3 (Sub-hiding and Sub-binding Commitment Schemes). *In the CRS model, under some standard assumptions, there exist commitment schemes that achieve sub-hiding and sub-binding.*

Proof. Basically all classic commitment schemes that do not require a particular setup phase and guarantee hiding and binding are a $\Pi_{com}^{2-party}$ commitment scheme. For instance, a commitment scheme built using a family of collision-resistant hash functions[4]. As a result, by considering the result of Lemma 2, all of them can also guarantee sub-hiding and sub-binding.   □

---

[4] A sample construction is available on https://cs.nyu.edu/courses/fall08/G22.3210-001/lect/lecture14.pdf.

5.3   Binding, Equivocality and Sub-hiding

Finally, we consider the last positive result in Table 1 which states that we can have a commitment to achieving hiding, equivocality, binding, and sub-hiding at the same time. In this result, we show that one can still achieve sub-hiding under standard assumptions by requiring that there exist hiding, binding, and equivocal commitment schemes.

Pedersen Commitment Scheme Achieves Sub-hiding. The Pedersen commitment scheme [Ped92] can guarantee sub-hiding property with minimal checking. The committer only needs to run the CKVer algorithm to verify ck before using the key for committing, and the check for this scheme is quite simple. Basically a committer needs to check whether both $g \neq 0$ and $h \neq 0$ before using $ck = (g, h)$.

Theorem 4 (Subversion-Resistant Pedersen Commitment). *The Pedersen commitment scheme with checking $g \neq 0$ and $h \neq 0$, satisfies hiding, equivocal, binding and sub-hiding under the discrete logarithm assumption in $\mathbb{G}$.*

Proof. For the sub-hiding property, once CKVer(gk, ck) returned 1, we conclude that both g and h are non-zero group elements, so one can notice that upon random choice of $r \in \mathbb{Z}_p$, for any $m \in \mathbb{Z}_p$, $c = g^m h^r$ is uniformly distributed over $\mathbb{G}$. For the binding property, as the non-subversion resistant version, one can observe that given openings (r_0, r_1) for a commitment c to distinct messages (m_0, m_1), the relation $g^{m_0} h^{r_0} = g^{m_1} h^{r_1}$ leads to $h = g^{\frac{m_0 - m_1}{r_1 - r_0}}$, which gives the discrete logarithm of h in base g. Intuitively, if the discrete logarithm problem is hard, the commitment scheme is (computationally) binding. For equivocality, as the original scheme, given trapdoor tk of the commitment key ck, one can generate a fake commitment and the corresponding valid opening.   □

Acknowledgment. This work was supported in part by the Estonian Research Council grant PRG49, by the Defense Advanced Research Projects Agency (DARPA) under Contract No. HR001120C0085, and by Cyber Security Research Flanders with reference number VR20192203. Any opinions, findings and conclusions or recommendations expressed in this material are those of the author(s) and do not necessarily reflect the views of the ERC, DARPA, the US Government or Cyber Security Research Flanders. The U.S. Government is authorized to reproduce and distribute reprints for governmental purposes notwithstanding any copyright annotation therein.

References

[ABK18] Auerbach, B., Bellare, M., Kiltz, E.: Public-key encryption resistant to parameter subversion and its realization from efficiently-embeddable groups. In: Abdalla, M., Dahab, R. (eds.) PKC 2018. LNCS, vol. 10769, pp. 348–377. Springer, Cham (2018). https://doi.org/10.1007/978-3-319-76578-5_12

[AMV15] Ateniese, G., Magri, B., Venturi, D.: Subversion-resilient signatures: Definitions, constructions and applications. Cryptology ePrint Archive, Report 2015/517 (2015). http://eprint.iacr.org/2015/517

[Bag19a] Baghery, K.: Subversion-resistant commitment schemes: definitions and constructions. Cryptology ePrint Archive, Report 2019/1065 (2019). https://eprint.iacr.org/2019/1065

[Bag19b] Baghery, K.: Subversion-resistant simulation (knowledge) sound NIZKs. In: Albrecht, M. (ed.) IMACC 2019. LNCS, vol. 11929, pp. 42–63. Springer, Cham (2019). https://doi.org/10.1007/978-3-030-35199-1_3

[BBG+13] Ball, J., Borger, J., Greenwald, G., et al.: Revealed: how US and UK spy agencies defeat internet privacy and security. Guard. **6**, 2–8 (2013)

[BCG+14] Ben-Sasson, E., et al.: ZeroCash: decentralized anonymous payments from bitcoin. In: 2014 IEEE Symposium on Security and Privacy, pp. 459–474. IEEE Computer Society Press, May 2014

[BFM88] Blum, M., Feldman, P., Micali, S.: Non-interactive zero-knowledge and its applications. In: STOC 1988, Chicago, Illinois, USA, 2–4 May 1988, pp. 103–112. ACM Press (1988)

[BFS16] Bellare, M., Fuchsbauer, G., Scafuro, A.: NIZKs with an untrusted CRS: security in the face of parameter subversion. In: Cheon, J.H., Takagi, T. (eds.) ASIACRYPT 2016. LNCS, vol. 10032, pp. 777–804. Springer, Heidelberg (2016). https://doi.org/10.1007/978-3-662-53890-6_26

[BGR98] Bellare, M., Garay, J.A., Rabin, T.: Batch verification with applications to cryptography and checking. In: Lucchesi, C.L., Moura, A.V. (eds.) LATIN 1998. LNCS, vol. 1380, pp. 170–191. Springer, Heidelberg (1998). https://doi.org/10.1007/BFb0054320

[Blu81] Blum, M.: Coin flipping by telephone. In: Gersho, A. (ed.) CRYPTO 1981, volume ECE Report 82–04, pp. 11–15. U.C. Santa Barbara, Department of Electronic and Computer Engineering (1981)

[BPR14] Bellare, M., Paterson, K.G., Rogaway, P.: Security of symmetric encryption against mass surveillance. In: Garay, J.A., Gennaro, R. (eds.) CRYPTO 2014. LNCS, vol. 8616, pp. 1–19. Springer, Heidelberg (2014). https://doi.org/10.1007/978-3-662-44371-2_1

[CIO98] Di Crescenzo, G., Ishai, Y., Ostrovsky, R.: Non-interactive and non-malleable commitment. In: Vitter, J.S. (ed.) STOC 1998, Dallas, Texas, USA, 23–26 May, pp. 141–150 (1998)

[Dam90] Damgård, I.B.: On the existence of bit commitment schemes and zero-knowledge proofs. In: Brassard, G. (ed.) CRYPTO 1989. LNCS, vol. 435, pp. 17–27. Springer, New York (1990). https://doi.org/10.1007/0-387-34805-0_3

[Dam92] Damgård, I.: Towards practical public key systems secure against chosen ciphertext attacks. In: Feigenbaum, J. (ed.) CRYPTO 1991. LNCS, vol. 576, pp. 445–456. Springer, Heidelberg (1992). https://doi.org/10.1007/3-540-46766-1_36

[DF02] Damgård, I., et al.: A statistically-hiding integer commitment scheme based on groups with hidden order. In: Zheng, Y. (ed.) ASIACRYPT 2002. LNCS, vol. 2501, pp. 125–142. Springer, Heidelberg (2002). https://doi.org/10.1007/3-540-36178-2_8

[EGL85] Even, S., Goldreich, O., Lempel, A.: A randomized protocol for signing contracts. Commun. ACM **28**(6), 637–647 (1985)

[Gab19] Gabizon, A.: On the security of the BCTV pinocchio ZK-snark variant. IACR Cryptology ePrint Archive 2019, 119 (2019)

[GL07] Groth, J., Lu, S.: Verifiable shuffle of large size ciphertexts. In: Okamoto, T., Wang, X. (eds.) PKC 2007. LNCS, vol. 4450, pp. 377–392. Springer, Heidelberg (2007). https://doi.org/10.1007/978-3-540-71677-8_25

[GMW87] Goldreich, O., Micali, S., Wigderson, A.: How to play any mental game or a completeness theorem for protocols with honest majority. In: STOC 1987, New York City, 25–27 May 1987, pp. 218–229 (1987)

[GMW91] Goldreich, O., Micali, S., Wigderson, A.: Proofs that yield nothing but their validity or all languages in NP have zero-knowledge proof systems. J. ACM 38(3), 691–729 (1991)

[GOS06] Groth, J., Ostrovsky, R., Sahai, A.: Non-interactive zaps and new techniques for NIZK. In: Dwork, C. (ed.) CRYPTO 2006. LNCS, vol. 4117, pp. 97–111. Springer, Heidelberg (2006). https://doi.org/10.1007/11818175_6

[GQ88] Guillou, L.C., Quisquater, J.-J.: A practical zero-knowledge protocol fitted to security microprocessor minimizing both transmission and memory. In: Barstow, D., et al. (eds.) EUROCRYPT 1988. LNCS, vol. 330, pp. 123–128. Springer, Heidelberg (1988). https://doi.org/10.1007/3-540-45961-8_11

[Gre14] Greenwald, G.: No place to hide: Edward Snowden, the NSA, and the US surveillance state. Macmillan (2014)

[Gro05] Groth, J.: Non-interactive zero-knowledge arguments for voting. In: Ioannidis, J., Keromytis, A., Yung, M. (eds.) ACNS 2005. LNCS, vol. 3531, pp. 467–482. Springer, Heidelberg (2005). https://doi.org/10.1007/11496137_32

[Gro09] Groth, J.: Homomorphic trapdoor commitments to group elements. Cryptology ePrint Archive, Report 2009/007 (2009). http://eprint.iacr.org/2009/007

[Gro10] Groth, J.: Short pairing-based non-interactive zero-knowledge arguments. In: Abe, M. (ed.) ASIACRYPT 2010. LNCS, vol. 6477, pp. 321–340. Springer, Heidelberg (2010). https://doi.org/10.1007/978-3-642-17373-8_19

[GS08] Groth, J., Sahai, A.: Efficient non-interactive proof systems for bilinear groups. In: Smart, N. (ed.) EUROCRYPT 2008. LNCS, vol. 4965, pp. 415–432. Springer, Heidelberg (2008). https://doi.org/10.1007/978-3-540-78967-3_24

[Hae19] Haenni, R.: Swiss post public intrusion test: Undetectable attack against vote integrity and secrecy (2019). https://e-voting.bfh.ch/app/download/7833162361/PIT2.pdf?t=1552395691

[HHK+17] Herold, G., Hoffmann, M., Klooß, M., Ràfols, C., Rupp, A.: New techniques for structural batch verification in bilinear groups with applications to groth-sahai proofs. In: Thuraisingham, B.M., Evans, D., Malkin, T., Xu, D. (eds.) ACM CCS 2017, pp.1547–1564. ACM Press, October/November 2017

[KMS+16] Kosba, A.E., Miller, A., Shi, E., Wen, Z., Papamanthou, C.: Hawk: the blockchain model of cryptography and privacy-preserving smart contracts. In: 2016 IEEE Symposium on Security and Privacy, pp. 839–858. IEEE Computer Society Press, May 2016

[Lip12] Lipmaa, H.: Progression-free sets and sublinear pairing-based non-interactive zero-knowledge arguments. In: Cramer, R. (ed.) TCC 2012. LNCS, vol. 7194, pp. 169–189. Springer, Heidelberg (2012). https://doi.org/10.1007/978-3-642-28914-9_10

[LPT19] Lewis, S.J., Pereira, O., Teague, V.: Trapdoor commitments in the swisspost e-voting shuffle proof (2019). https://people.eng.unimelb.edu.au/vjteague/SwissVote

[Nao91] Naor, M.: Bit commitment using pseudorandom generators. J. Cryptology 4(2), 151–158 (1991)

[Ped92]   Pedersen, T.P.: Non-interactive and information-theoretic secure verifiable secret sharing. In: Feigenbaum, J. (ed.) CRYPTO 1991. LNCS, vol. 576, pp. 129–140. Springer, Heidelberg (1992). https://doi.org/10.1007/3-540-46766-1_9

[PLS13]   Perlroth, N., Larson, J., Shane, S.: NSA able to foil basic safeguards of privacy on web. The New York Times, 5 (2013)

[Wik09]   Wikström, D.: A commitment-consistent proof of a shuffle. In: Boyd, C., González Nieto, J. (eds.) ACISP 2009. LNCS, vol. 5594, pp. 407–421. Springer, Heidelberg (2009). https://doi.org/10.1007/978-3-642-02620-1_28

Challenges in IT Security Processes and Solution Approaches with Process Mining

Aynesh Sundararaj[1], Silvia Knittl[2](✉) [iD], and Jens Grossklags[1] [iD]

[1] Technical University of Munich, Munich, Germany
sundararaj@tum.de, jens.grossklags@in.tum.de
[2] PricewaterhouseCoopers GmbH WPG, Munich, Germany
silvia.knittl@pwc.com

Abstract. Process mining is a rapidly developing field of data science currently focusing on business processes. The approach involves many techniques that may contribute to cyber security analysis as well. In particular, the measurement of deviations from a defined process is a central topic in process mining, and could find application in the context of IT security.

In this paper, we present a solution approach for IT security with process mining, which is based on experiments that we conducted on an Identity and Access Management (IAM) scenario. We have designed and implemented an appropriate lifelike environment and use cases to demonstrate both the suitability and limitations of process mining for cyber security processes. While process mining can detect deviations from cyber processes very well, not all deviations are relevant for security. Thus, more research on how to incorporate threat analysis into process mining will be necessary in the future.

Keywords: IT Security Process · Process mining · Conformance checking

1 Introduction

A comprehensive Enterprise Security Architecture consists of several coherent layers, including security domains, security services, or security products and tools [19]. In the ISO/IEC 27001 standard, information security is defined via the IT protection goals availability, integrity and confidentiality. Further factors of information security can be authenticity, accountability, non-repudiation and reliability [10]. To contextualize the IT protection goals, the standard considers security domains such as physical and environmental security, access control (Identity and Access Management, IAM) or business continuity management. Each security domain consists of different capabilities, such as identity, account or credential life cycle management in the IAM context. Those capabilities are implemented by one or more tools to support the underlying processes. The usage of these tools leaves traces in the form of log files. To achieve the protection goals,

© Springer Nature Switzerland AG 2020
K. Markantonakis and M. Petrocchi (Eds.): STM 2020, LNCS 12386, pp. 123–138, 2020.
https://doi.org/10.1007/978-3-030-59817-4_8

organizations usually use security information and event management (SIEM) systems that collect and examine these log files. This examination should identify deviations from the norm and trigger appropriate actions. Patterns are used for this purpose, recently supported by artificial intelligence. Very often this analysis happens within an isolated security domain or tool view. While the processes span several tool boundaries, there are hardly any end-to-end process views of the different security domains considered. However, deviations can be indicative of harmful behavior in these scenarios.

In business process management, the topic of process mining has seen a steady increase of popularity (see, e.g., [4]). Primary use cases of using process mining are finding process bottlenecks, process optimization, compliance and auditing. Therefore, commercial tools such as Celonis [5] integrate already by default the analysis of business processes like procurement or order processes that are implemented by standard business software (e.g., SAP systems). Both in business processes and in IT security processes, the human perspective is taken into account in the design for interaction, collaboration, coordination, or cooperation [14]. However, in the field of information security, humans are not only characterized as users and defenders, but also as potential attackers [11]. Both intentional (attacker) and unintentional (user, defender) misconduct can, therefore, lead to cyber incidents and must be considered in the analysis.

While many non-security business processes are standardized to the extent that they can be implemented using off-the-shelf software, there are hardly any such standardized IT security processes developed and established in different companies in a comparable way. Further, related academic work is sparse. One exception is Haufe et al. [8] who propose a high-level process framework for an Information Security Management System (ISMS) which could be a starting point for process implementation. One key reason for having such a high-level approach during security process implementations is, as we will show using the example of IAM, that in practice several tools are used for implementing one capability and the cyber processes go beyond tool boundaries. Further, the implementation characteristics depend on the respective compliance requirements and risk appetite of the organization. For example, access to applications can be granted without or with approval steps or even with a 4-eyes or 6-eyes principle.

Applying process mining in the security context also matches a broader trend. For example, according to Schinagl and Shahim [18], it is only recently that security shifts "from a narrow-focused isolated issue towards a strategic business issue." The authors conclude in their study that traditional IT security approaches based on rather static security controls and common practices will be insufficient in the future due to the fast and agile changes in IT. Compliance checking and auditing are already an integral part of cyber security analysis, thus process mining can be considered as a natural choice as one of the methods for the future. But the application in the field of cyber security related problems is not yet common. This observation fosters our motivation to study how we can use process mining in the context of a specific but highly relevant cyber security scenario.

On a high level, process mining can be summarized as follows: Event logs describing the events and activities happening in a (business) process are required by the process mining algorithm. Both the input and output here are process models, which can be represented by a Petri net, a tree or graph describing the process flow. However, there is no clear definition or methodology on how to use process mining techniques in the context of cyber security processes.

One of the main goals is, therefore, to identify techniques of process mining that are suitable for cyber security process analysis and to study how to effectively use them. We address the following guiding research questions:

1. What aspects of the process mining technique are usable for cyber security process analysis?
2. What kind of problems related to cyber security processes can be solved using process mining? How can those problems be solved and what are the requirements and execution steps?
3. What are the metrics that measure the execution and results? How to use the results from a cyber security viewpoint for further analysis?

Keeping these research questions in mind, we formulate a case study with a scientific approach based on the guidelines from Runeson and Höst [16]. More specifically, in Sect. 2, we describe an example cyber process scenario within the IAM domain and outline the associated security requirements. This process scenario will be the foundation for our case that we prepare using an experimental approach. Section 3 outlines an overview of related work. In Sect. 4, we explain how process mining can be used to tackle the requirements retrieved from our IAM process and we show results based on our experiments. We conclude with a summary and discussion of limitations of our approach in Sect. 5.

2 Background: Cyber Process Scenario

In order to identify what aspects of process mining are suitable for cyber security process analysis and what kind of problems it can solve, a subset of processes in the domain of IAM is selected as an example scenario for the sake of brevity. We had no real user data available for our research in which we could test our approaches. Therefore, we built an adequate demo environment ourselves. We equipped this environment with a typical tool set, which can be found in a real company environment as well, and which also depicts processes that go beyond several tool boundaries (see Sect. 4.1). By designing the environment in this way, we have ensured that our test cases correspond to real cases.

IAM can be described as a collection of methods, tools and processes to allocate, manage and revert identity and accesses to the resources of an organization [20]. According to Damon and Coetzee [6], IAM should fulfill the following requirements in order to be effective and useful: legal and regulatory compliance, information access everywhere, access protection/accountability, operational efficiency, cross organization integration, cost reduction, risk management, end-user experience. In the scope of cyber security, any activity which deviates from a standard process should be considered a candidate for malicious behavior. Our purpose was to identify process mining methodologies and solutions for detecting such malicious and inefficient workflows.

Figure 1 shows in a highly simplified fashion the IAM capabilities such as identity, account and credential life cycle management and possible applications for the technical implementation of these capabilities (such as an IAM system), or an account store (such as a directory service). A selection of IAM process activities are shown, such as 'New Joiner', 'Leaver' or 'New Account'. The process activities are interconnected. A new joiner in the HR-System triggers the creation of a new identity in the IAM tool. This in turn triggers the creation of a new account combined with the generation of a new credential in the account or credential store.

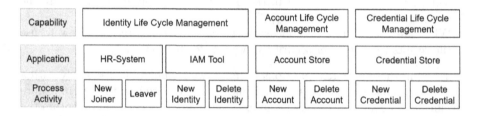

Fig. 1. IAM capabilities, applications and process activities (excerpt, simplified)

Figure 2 depicts a high level reference IAM process which was used in our case study. The reference process distinguishes users broadly as managers and other users, like employees. It also shows various sub-process flows indicating which actions of an employee or a manager can proceed. We can also see that some of the process flows can involve the same request processed by multiple applications. We define *process slip* as an activity where the set of operations will continue from one software setup to another. For example, any access request will be raised at the IAM tool. Once it is approved, the IAM tool will forward the action to the account store to enable access to the specific request. Since this process is highly complex and may have lapses, which could be misused, this should be recognized by mining the system-wide process of the organization.

The message even from such a simple process diagram is that processes can be highly complex, may involve multiple heterogeneous communications, actions and various applications.

3 Related Work

The state of the art of IT security anomaly detection solutions can be mainly categorized into vulnerability scanners, intrusion prevention systems and intrusion detection systems [15]. Most of these solutions are protecting systems against network level threats and offer only very limited applicability against application

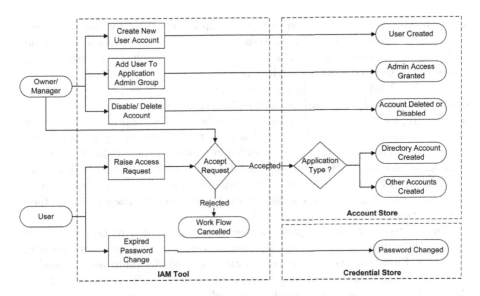

Fig. 2. IAM Reference Process used for this work

or business process level threats. Cyber security analysis of business processes using process mining can be one such perspective to look at application level threats, to understand possible threats, and to establish strict event execution patterns within the process flows.

Recent work by Sarno et al. [17] fits in this area. The authors propose a hybrid of process mining and data mining techniques to detect fraud in ERP systems. The authors use a simulated credit application process dataset from previous research. Our approach is different from their work. We consider the idea of a reference process and use of conformance checking to validate the security of the processes. We make use of our data aggregator program to generate a dataset for process mining such that process mining techniques can pinpoint these anomalies. We also heavily focus on security related processes within a real life demo environment and consider the concept of process slip.

Accorsi and Stocker [2] discuss how process mining can be used for security investigations if structured and meaningful logs are available. The authors put forward a simulated case study from security audits in the financial sector. However, a real life environment and security related processes need a different approach. Because the event logs extracted out of these systems provide very minimal details, the methodology and the analysis provided by the authors cannot be used for these kinds of event logs due to a lack of information for the proposed method. Also the idea of process slip was not considered. Complex systems have processes flowing across multiple applications to complete one request. Therefore, it is important to be able to analyze these complex processes in the form of process graphs to see if there any possible security issues and efficiency shortcomings. This can be visualized by mining the system-wide process within an organization. The simulation of process slip is important for our case study and more relevant for security analysis because the chances of security issues with respect to processes is higher in a distributed (multi-tool) environment compared to isolated software environments.

Van der Aalst and de Medeiros illustrate the usage of process mining to detect anomalies [1]. The authors discuss how to use an alpha-algorithm to mine process graphs from financial data and to subsequently conduct security audit analysis with conformance checking. Using a real life case study from a Dutch municipality, they show that the traces having a trace fitness below 0.80 can be considered anomalous. However, substantial uncertainties and unknowns remain, which is not fully adequate for security applications. We propose a process mining algorithm and conformance checking with a different approach to avoid these uncertainties.

The limited past research primarily focuses on anomaly detection and fails to capture difficulties in process mining, specifically in real-life-like software environments. First, modern software environments consist of multiple independent tools and applications. The logs generated by modern applications are independent and they necessitate methods to consolidate and generate a single event log for process mining analysis. Second, there is only limited analysis to evaluate core process mining techniques as a key solution for cyber security process mining. Considering these factors, we propose a systematic method to use process mining for cyber security analysis. In the case of cyber security, this can be understood as a new class of defense and forensic methods. For our work, we use existing process mining and conformance checking algorithms from the scientific literature, and apply them to the security context.

Taking a step away from the process mining literature, the classical event log-based intrusion detection typically follows text pattern analysis using various methods that typically do not consider the control flow of systems. For example, the research from Yang and Jie [12] describes one such system. The intrusion detection system collects real-time event data logs from various computers present in the system and analyzes the collected logs for malicious activity using data mining techniques. The fundamental difference between these techniques and process mining methods are that process mining follows a strict control flow based analysis.

Finally, we apply the concept of *cost-based analysis for conformance checking*, which was used for conformance checking of process models [3]. Based on the cost-based replay of event logs against process models and assigning a cost to tasks in the process, we can quantitatively say how significantly an event log deviates from the reference process. The algorithm uses the A* shortest path-finding algorithm from graph theory, and gives a detailed explanation of the cost-based Petri net conformance checking algorithm. The technique penalizes traces for skipping or inserting activities and is also based on the costs of the activities. The method is useful in the security context, because it acknowledges that some tasks are more important than others. In particular, the concept of 'weight' can be very useful because the impact of skipping or inserting specific activities may vary from activity to activity. The algorithm selects the best matching (i.e., lowest cost) instance in case of skipping or inserting tasks based on weights.

The above introduced concepts partially build the basis for the concept, experimentation and results described in the following.

4 Process Mining in Cyber Security

We describe the demo environment in Sect. 4.1 and our experimental approach in Sect. 4.2. The execution of the experiments and results are shown in Sect. 4.3.

4.1 Demo Environment Setup

Figure 3 outlines the architecture of the demo environment with the goal to simulate an IAM environment. It consists of two applications: one IAM tool and one directory service, which closely matches real life IAM deployments. More specifically, we used one off-the-shelf IAM software and a directory service that acts both as an account and credential store. The IAM software communicates with the directory and other subsystems using its own Windows services, RPC calls or web services.

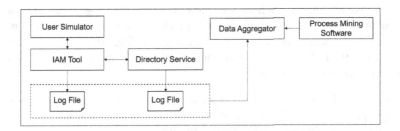

Fig. 3. Demo environment architecture

We specifically developed a user simulator and a data aggregator for this research. The user simulator is a component allowing to simulate user behavior; since there exist (to the best of our knowledge) no suitable publicly available IAM audit logs. The main idea is to create a test infrastructure that simulates the IAM process with this setup. The core functionality and configuration of the demo environment:

a) consists of a defined number of internal artificial users of an organization,
b) simulates IAM related activities like creation of a new identity or account,
c) focuses on internal users and violation of the policy of internal users,
d) simulates approval of access to resources, account creation and deletion, and
e) simulates several business workflows of internal work items of an organization.

The dataset generation for this case study focused on simulating an end-to-end IAM process using dummy users. Later, the suspicious malicious behaviors were manually embedded into the system in order to demonstrate the effectiveness of the conformance checking step. The dataset with no malicious behavior is classified as a training dataset, and the dataset with embedded malicious behavior is classified as a test dataset.

The data aggregation program was developed to collect and consolidate event logs for process mining purposes. There are several things to consider when trying to combine multiple log files from different applications into one event log. Briefly, they are filtering and converting the columns of each log entry into an event log trace and finding mapping fields for case identifiers across these logs, in order to see the process control flow from one software system to another. We also generate the task names from the individual logs by appending role names to tasks. This way, we can also see if the tasks are executed by the right roles during conformance checking. We present only the results related to inserted or skipped activities in this paper.

4.2 Experimentation Overview

We take up the previously mentioned goals of IAM in our design of the experiments, e.g., the IAM process allows cross-organization integration and access protection/accountability. Process models can be also considered as a solution for associated challenges such as silo view, missing business focus and lack of overview of the system. The techniques and ideas used in this work are mainly conformance checking and STRIDE[1] threat modelling at an activity level of each process [9]. Below are some of the techniques that can be used to verify and secure security-related processes.

– By using conformance checking, we can verify if the process complies to the desired process or not. Any deviations from the desired process can be taken up for the investigation and explored further.
– By using threat modeling techniques at each activity in a process, we can tell if a process is secure or not. This will still involve manual work.
– Additionally, it can be checked if the process conforms to process standards defined by security standards such as ISO:IEC 27001.

In our work, we primarily demonstrate the viability of conformance based process security checking, which already provides some level of automation in analyzing process security. Follow-up analysis tasks, i.e., STRIDE analysis and ISO standard related techniques, remain manual analysis. As outlined in Fig. 4, the following steps are performed in the experiment:

---

[1] The acronym STRIDE stands for the following six threat categories: **S**poofing identity, **T**ampering with data, **R**epudiation (Non-repudiation), **I**nformation disclosure, **D**enial of service and **E**levation of privilege.

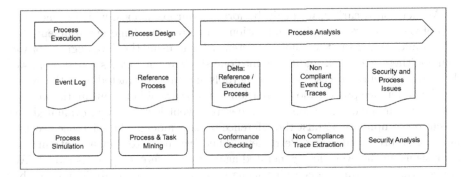

Fig. 4. The steps of the experiment

- Event Log Generation: We generate the event log by using the User Simulator created for the demo environment that we had installed and configured for this experiment.
- Process Mining and Task Mining: To develop a reference process, we use process and task mining to identify existing process flows and tasks/activities in the system.
- Conformance Checking: Once we have a reference process, we embed malicious situations and simulate the demo environment. Then, we conduct conformance checking of event logs against the reference process.
- Non-compliant Trace Extraction: After conformance checking, we extract the non-compliant traces from the test event log, performing conformance checking against our reference process model.
- Security Analysis: We analyze the non-compliant traces for security and process flaws.

4.3   Experiment Execution and Results

The primary output of the process and task mining is a process graph which is represented as a Petri net. In our case, the Petri net shows the multiple paths of process flows as per the real system. The graphic is too large to be displayed here. Therefore we have divided it into three parts and show them in Fig. 5 in the Appendix. The graph shows the different paths and process steps that can occur in the IAM process. The most common example is the account creation process which starts from the IAM tool and continues through the directory tool. The Petri net also shows the mandatory tasks that need to be initiated for successful progress on each step. The tasks represented in the Petri net, which are prefixed with 'SP', are tasks related to the IAM tool and the tasks prefixed with 'AD' are tasks related to the directory services tool.

As mentioned earlier, we begin by forming our event logs, which is the first step of the experiment. Using simulation data from the demo environment, we extract audit logs from the different systems. Then, using the data aggregator we combine these extracted audit logs into one single event log. As a first step, we develop a reference process model using tools and tasks extracted from the event log. The reference process model creation is a mixture of both automatic process mining and manual alteration. The generated event logs are then evaluated for execution compliance against the reference process model. The reference process model is represented using Petri nets. Then, we need to run a conformance analysis using the event logs generated against the reference process model. We applied the 'conformance checking using cost-based fitness analysis' for this by using two datasets. One named training dataset that was used to extract the process model. The other dataset is called the test dataset, which contains the inserted malicious situations.

Depending on the context, skipping or inserting a particular activity in a process execution can be very dangerous compared to others. For example, a newly found 'delete' activity can be more dangerous compared to an activity such as 'save again'. For distinguishing such executions based on the varied severity of the nature of the activities/events, we used the weight-based approach. We configured weights for each activity transition based on the severity of the activity. These values are used by the algorithm to calculate fitness. For each activity or task, corresponding weights for log move or model move are shown here. The algorithm takes care of penalizing based on inserting or skipping activities. The technique cost based replay analysis is applied for the conformance checking. As mentioned earlier, we configured weights for transition of activities based on the severity of the activity. The activities that have higher significance on non-compliance scenarios are assigned higher weights compared to other activities. Based on the weights of the activities, we can also understand the severity of the compliance quantitatively.

In order to simulate the capturing of malicious activities, some accounts in the directory were manually deleted. Then, we ran a conformance check against the test data cases and reference model. The output were cases, i.e., the corresponding set of event logs, and their trace fitness to the given reference model. The traces containing the activities related to these deletions are included in the test dataset. In terms of conformance checking this is an inserted behavior, because the new set of activities are inserted into the control flow of the process model. However, the corresponding reference model does not exhibit a control flow containing these newly inserted activities in any sub process flow.

All the traces which contain the directory account deletion fall below a trace fitness value of 1 as expected. Based on the behavior of the inserted variations, the trace value changed according to the basis of the weights we had previously assigned to the activities. After execution of the conformance checking algorithm, we found 40 cases failing to meet a trace fitness of 1.00. Breaking down those 40 out of 121 cases, the following technical issues were found:

6 (out of 40) failed directory provisions, 29 (out of 40) bugs in process execution, 5 (out of 40) manual deletions of accounts. Further exploring them, we can see that 6 out of 11 of them got deleted at the same timestamp as the accounts were created. A cross check for provisioning failure records in the IAM software showed, that the accounts which were deleted automatically by the IAM software have a provisioning failure record and accounts that are assumed to be manually deleted do not have any provisioning failure record. This experiment showed that by applying the above mentioned steps it is possible to capture the deletion scenario. But still additional information is needed to distinguish between software driven deletion and manual deletion.

We enhanced our experiment to automate if the tasks are security related or not using the task name attribute. This helps us to focus on security related tasks extracted from these logs and exclude other tasks or unimportant process flows. This enhancement could be also used for automatic weight allocation for tasks in the future. We started by applying a natural language processing (NLP) technique as an initial strategy (see, e.g., Word2Vec in [13]). NLP techniques can be used to identify similarity between 2 words if trained using the right kind of documents. We can use Word2Vec for identifying if a word is related to security or not using similarity analysis. To automate the malicious process execution detection, we can also use some of the NLP techniques. As an extension part for the above experimentation, a word similarity check was tried using word2vec and a pre-trained model from Google. We evaluated the tasks mined against the word 'security' for word similarity, and could see that as anticipated the words related to security were showing higher similarity scores compared to words not related to security. Reporting the results of this effort is, however, beyond the scope of this paper.

5   Summary

In this section, we briefly summarize the application of process mining techniques on cyber security processes using the results of the case study presented above and also discuss challenges and limitations as well as future research questions. We addressed the main questions of this case study:

1) The capabilities and effectiveness of process mining methods for cyber security processes: In this article, we demonstrated based on an experimental approach that process mining and conformance checking techniques can be applied in the context of cyber security processes based on the example of IAM. It was demonstrated that it is very much suited for process control flow conformance checking. We also showed how to use cost-based replay of the log for conformance checking using our case study. When applying conformance checking techniques on a structured event log based on a very well designed process model of a security process, the occurrence of different and therefore potentially harmful behaviors can be discovered. Such differences can be due to inefficiency in the process or security lapses, hence process mining can be helpful in discovering these lapses. What we can do is understand the current business process and mine tasks. Using the mined tasks and sub-process control flows, we can design a process, utilizing conformance analysis based on replay to evaluate if the system is performing as per expectation or not. Any traces which are not compliant can be analyzed for malicious process executions. The reference process needs to be designed carefully and involves human participation. We have to develop guidelines in future work for aspects to be considered while designing a reference process to reduce errors.

2) The limitations of process mining for cyber security processes: Our research is at the starting point for reasoning on the subject of process mining in cyber security processes. For the experiments, we generated data sets that are based on a demo environment instead of real life data sets. When designing our demo environment, we ensured that it has a setup that is typically used in a corporate context. Thus, our case study suggests that they indeed can be helpful in cyber security analysis. In the future, applying these techniques on real life data is recommended.

Some limitations to these techniques exist for applying them in cyber security processes. One is that some of the analysis of these lapses is still manual. Another limitation of conformance checking is that an additional analysis of the original log files is needed to identify the actual issue; process mining can only tell if there is an issue or not. A further expansion of the demo environment by adding more suitable security analysis tools can reduce the amount of manual work. The extent to which SIEM tools interact appropriately with process mining tools could be investigated for this purpose in the future.

In our approach, we used a reference process model that was generated by using process mining. In case such a reference process model is extracted from a compromised log, the security analysis could fail. Further, process mining cannot cover all software vulnerabilities. It can only cover process flaws or events that are logged. In case an attacker can fit her attack within a process flow, this can currently not be detected by conformance checking of process mining. According to the STRIDE model, there are various attack possibilities to intervene in a process in a damaging way. The isolated tampering with data, such as changing data in one place without utilizing the intended process tools and sequences, can be detected by process mining as shown above. Intentional or unintentional malicious behavior of a user or a hacker might be detected by process mining. For this purpose, future research in the field of real time process mining should be undertaken.

In our example, a denial of service attack by a malicious user who can fit her attack within a process flow would be possible, for example, through mass deletion of access rights in the IAM tool. In addition to the implementation of counter measures directly in the process or within the IAM tool, *real time* process mining could also be useful to detect such malicious behavior. This was beyond the scope of our study. To investigate if other types of attacks like spoofing an identity or elevation of privileges can be identified by process mining, further studies about how to integrate process mining with current security methods should be conducted.

3) The metrics that measure the execution and results and how to use the results from a cyber security viewpoint for further analysis and research: To measure the detection of mismatches between the process specification and the execution of a particular process instance, trace fitness is an appropriate instrument. While we see the outcomes of our study quite promising, future work could enhance the automation to select the traces that need to be analyzed in order to reduce human effort and potential error. New techniques in the areas of conformance checking, such as multi-perspective conformance checking [7], could be worth to explore for cyber security process analysis. These techniques can consider additional information apart from event logs to do conformance checking. Also the application of threat modelling on processes for each activity can be overwhelming suggesting a need for automation.

With our approach, we have laid a first foundation on the applicability of process mining in the area of cyber security processes. We consider the approach to be a promising addition to established security methods. Our case study leads to several additional future research questions that need to be answered like performing a comparative study of conformance checking techniques on cyber security processes and work on the automation of processing identified malicious audits.

Acknowledgements. We thank the anonymous reviewers for their helpful comments.

A   Appendix

In the Appendix, we show the three parts of the graphs of the Petri net in Figure 5.

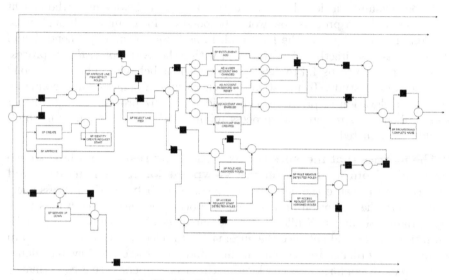

Part 1 of 3 of the Petri net output

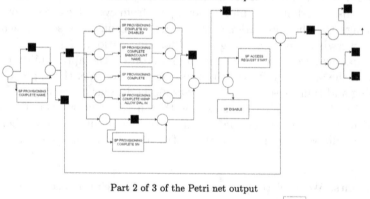

Part 2 of 3 of the Petri net output

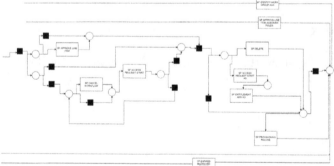

Part 3 of 3 of the Petri net output

Fig. 5. Petri net output

References

1. van der Aalst, W., de Medeiros, A.: Process mining and security: detecting anomalous process executions and checking process conformance. In: Proceedings of the 2nd International Workshop on Security Issues with Petri Nets and other Computational Models (WISP 2004), pp. 3–21 (2005)
2. Accorsi, R., Stocker, T.: On the exploitation of process mining for security audits: the conformance checking case. In: Proceedings of the 27th Annual ACM Symposium on Applied Computing, SAC 2012, pp. 1709–1716. ACM, New York (2012). https://doi.org/10.1145/2245276.2232051
3. Adriansyah, A., van Dongen, B., van der Aalst, W.: Conformance checking using cost-based fitness analysis. In: Proceedings of the IEEE 15th International Enterprise Distributed Object Computing Conference, pp. 55–64 (2011). https://doi.org/10.1109/EDOC.2011.12
4. Ailenei, I., Rozinat, A., Eckert, A., van der Aalst, W.M.P.: Definition and validation of process mining use cases. In: Daniel, F., Barkaoui, K., Dustdar, S. (eds.) BPM 2011. LNBIP, vol. 99, pp. 75–86. Springer, Heidelberg (2012). https://doi.org/10.1007/978-3-642-28108-2_7
5. Celonis SE: Celonis (2020). www.celonis.com. Accessed 07 May 2020
6. Damon, F., Coetzee, M.: Towards a generic identity and access assurance model by component analysis - A conceptual review. In: Proceedings of the First International Conference on Enterprise Systems: ES 2013, pp. 1–11, Nov 2013. https://doi.org/10.1109/ES.2013.6690086
7. Dunzer, S., Stierle, M., Matzner, M., Baier, S.: Conformance checking: a state-of-the-art literature review. In: Proceedings of the 11th International Conference on Subject-Oriented Business Process Management. S-BPM ONE 2019. Association for Computing Machinery, New York (2019). https://doi.org/10.1145/3329007.3329014
8. Haufe, K., Colomo-Palacios, R., Dzombeta, S., Brandis, K., Stantchev, V.: A process framework for information security management. Int. J. Inf. Syst. Project Manage. **04**, 27–47 (2016)
9. Hernan, S., Lambert, S., Ostwald, T., Shostack, A.: Threat modeling - uncover security design flaws using the stride approach. MSDN Magazine, November 2009. https://web.archive.org/web/20070303103639/, http://msdn.microsoft.com/msdnmag/issues/06/11/ThreatModeling/default.aspx
10. ISO: ISO/IEC 27001:2013: Standard, International Organization for Standardization, Geneva, CH, October 2013
11. King, Z., Henshel, D., Flora, L., Cains, M.G., Hoffman, B., Sample, C.: Characterizing and measuring maliciousness for cybersecurity risk assessment. Front. Psychol. (2018), https://www.ncbi.nlm.nih.gov/pmc/articles/PMC5807417/
12. Li, Y., Li, J.: Study of cloud computing security and application in safe city. Appl. Mech. Mater. 738–739, 299–303 (2015). https://doi.org/10.4028/www.scientific.net/AMM.738-739.299
13. Mikolov, T., Chen, K., Corrado, G., Dean, J.: Efficient estimation of word representations in vector space. arXiv preprint arXiv:1301.3781 (2013)
14. Nurcan, S., Schmidt, R.: Theme section of BPMDS 2014: the human perspective in business processes. Softw. Syst. Model. **16**(3), 627–629 (2016). https://doi.org/10.1007/s10270-016-0570-9

15. Razzaq, A., Hur, A., Ahmad, H.F., Masood, M.: Cyber security: threats, reasons, challenges, methodologies and state of the art solutions for industrial applications. In: IEEE Eleventh International Symposium on Autonomous Decentralized Systems (ISADS), pp. 1–6 (2013)

16. Runeson, P., Höst, M.: Guidelines for conducting and reporting case study research in software engineering. Empir. Software Eng. **14**, 131–164 (2009). https://doi.org/10.1007/s10664-008-9102-8

17. Sarno, R., Sinaga, F., Sungkono, K.R.: Anomaly detection in business processes using process mining and fuzzy association rule learning. J. Big Data **7**(1), 1–19 (2020). https://doi.org/10.1186/s40537-019-0277-1

18. Schinagl, S., Shahim, A.: What do we know about information security governance? "From the basement to the boardroom": towards digital security governance. Inf. Comput. Secur. (2020). https://www.emerald.com/insight/content/doi/10.1108/ICS-02-2019-0033/full/html

19. Sherwood, J., Clark, A., Lynas, D.: Enterprise Security Architecture: A Business-Driven Approach. CMP Books (2005)

20. Thakur, M.A., Gaikwad, R.: User identity and access management trends in IT infrastructure - an overview. In: International Conference on Pervasive Computing (ICPC), pp. 1–4, January 2015. https://doi.org/10.1109/PERVASIVE.2015.7086972

Author Index

Printed in the United States
by Bookmasters

Printed in the United States
By Bookmasters